Milongas

Edgardo Cozarinsky

With a preface by Alberto Manguel

Translated from the Spanish by Valerie Miles

archipelago books

Library of Congress Cataloging-in-Publication Data available upon request

Archipelago Books
232 3rd Street #A111
Brooklyn, NY 11215
www.archipelagobooks.org

Distributed by Penguin Random House
www.penguinrandomhouse.com

Cover art: Men posing in Argentina in the 1900s

This work was made possible by the New York State Council on the Arts with the support of
Governor Andrew M. Cuomo and the New York State Legislature. Funding for the translation
of this book was provided by a grant from the Carl Lesnor Family Foundation.

Work published within the framework of "Sur" Translation Support Program
of the Ministry of Foreign Affairs and Worship of the Argentine Republic.
Obra editada en el marco del Programa "Sur" de Apoyo a las Traducciones
del Ministerio de Relaciones Exteriores y Culto de la República Argentina.

Archipelago Books also gratefully acknowledges the generous support from
Lannan Foundation, the National Endowment for the Arts,
and the New York City Department of Cultural Affairs.

PRINTED IN THE UNITED STATES OF AMERICA

Perhaps no other music lends itself to reverie like tango.
It enters your being and possesses it wholly, like a narcotic.
Its rhythm allows you to suspend thought, and frees the soul
to float inside the body . . .

Ezequiel Martínez Estrada

In memory of Julio Nudler

Table of Contents

Preface

Apparently (but etymologies are unreliable) the word "milonga" derives from an African word meaning "word." Jorge Luis Borges, in an early text, attributed the birth of the milonga and the tango to the arrival of African slaves: "the habanera mother of the tango, the candombe..." Since in its remote beginnings the milonga was sung, the singing of words, an adjunct to the music, became the name by which the milonga was known. Popular singers, "payadores," played milongas on the guitar, to which later, at social gatherings, the violin, the flute, and the piano were added. And yet, in the same way that the word "scribe" in ancient Mesopotamia concealed the fact that the main power of the scribe was not to write but to read, to decipher the messages preserved on the clay tablet, the name "milonga" concealed the fact that the milonga was above all not words but music.

Perhaps because music precedes words, or does not require them in order to exist, the succession of notes lends itself readily as a symbol of the emotional state of its listener or performer. Nothing in a certain beat, a certain rhythm, a certain tune carries an explicit emotive label: as in Bishop Berkeley's philosophy, the emotion in the milonga lies in the performance or in the reception of that performance, as the taste and color of an apple is in the tongue that tastes it and the eye that sees it.

A word or an image belong to a given vocabulary. Music adapts itself to the context given to it and acquires in the process a specific identity: melancholy, stirring, quarrelsome, sensuous. The tango, especially for a "porteño," for a native of Buenos Aires, can be all those things at once. The milonga, a term that can be used for the tango that is not merely played or sung but danced, is above all sensuous, even lascivious, certainly erotic. The tango can be naïve or mawkish; the milonga is never innocent. On the contrary, it is (in the eye and ear of the beholder) alluring, sexual, magnetic, suggesting an undercurrent of danger and possibly violence. "This book's title is *Milongas* and not *Tangos*," Cozarinsky sternly states. "Its focus is on the dance, not the music." Music translated into movement, channeled through movement outside the verbal realm. Style is, according to Cozarinsky, the inescapable essence of milonga. "If we define style as the individual response of one body to the sound of the music," he says, "then that style will express itself and continue being refined until it grows splendid in some cases, merely correct in others, or else remains dull. In milonga, the dance and the dancer are indistinguishable from the very first step."

Cozarinsky traces the milonga (and in its wake, the tango) throughout the twentieth century and across several continents. He finds milongas danced in Kraków, London, Moscow, New York, Tokyo, and discovers that the movements of the dance can be learned and brilliantly performed by unexpected people, from the couple that danced for the censorious Pope Pius X to that archetypal Latin lover, Rudolfo Valentino, in *The Four Horsemen of the Apocalypse*; from the *belle époque* icons Gabriele D'Annunzio and Ida Rubinstein to the chauvinistic French President Raymond Poincaré and his wife. Cozarinsky is not a distant observer: he is an experienced practitioner of the art, a well-known figure in the popular joints in which milonga is danced today in Buenos Aires. His essay has something of an autobiographical confession.

Unlike other dances, especially those born in the twentieth century, in the milonga youth and physical beauty are not weighty qualities. The dancers can be old and stout, short or tall: nothing matters except the skill with which their body conjures up or follows a style. If the dancers don't follow the adamant rules of style, they are not dancing milonga. Traditionally, men and women fulfilled different roles in the dance; today, same-sex couples dancing a milonga have to agree on who is playing one role or the other. Jack Lemmon in drag, with a rose between the teeth, stumbles around the dance floor in the arms of Joe E. Brown who has to correct Lemmon's style: "Daphne, you're leading again."

National identities are imaginary constructs and yet, because of certain emotions associated with certain nationalities, music can acquire a kind of passport that assigns it to a particular country. Country or city: milonga is the music of Buenos Aires, not Argentina; it is "porteño," endemic to Buenos Aires, and becomes Argentinian only because Buenos Aires is the metonym for the nation. It is commonplace to say that the sound of a milonga makes a porteño weep with nostalgia. Cozarinsky makes it clear that the milonga is above all an existential condition, an ineffable, impassioned state of being.

Alberto Manguel
Lisbon, May 13 2021

Milongas

The First Move

O body swayed to music, O brightening glance,
How can we know the dancer from the dance?

W. B. Yeats, "Among School Children"

This book's title is *Milongas* and not *Tangos*.

Its focus is on the dance, not the music.

And the ways the dance is staged: the scenes, the rituals, and above all else, the characters.

In keeping with the great Irish poet's insight on the impossibility of distinguishing between the dance and the dancer, the first thing a visitor to a milonga observes is how the music seems to dictate different figures to each couple. The movements of one pair on the dance floor rarely coincide with another's at the same musical moment.

The notion of style in danced tango, it seems to me, is not so much an end as it is an inescapable condition. Whatever is suggested by the music, even to the most tentative beginner, is suggested to him or her alone. If we define style as the individual response of one body to the sound of the music, then that style will express itself and continue being refined until it grows splendid in some cases, merely correct in others, or else remains dull. In milonga, the dance and the dancer are indistinguishable from the very first step.

The blank looks or expressions of effort and concentration on the dancers' faces, in place of stage masks, mesmerize the first-time visitor to a milonga; and tiny details, like pictures, can have sweeping connotations: a pair of street shoes, for example, a token of daily life left under the table by a woman who steps into her tango shoes and onto the dance floor, gliding into her imaginary life.

The renewed popularity of tango dancing, far removed now from the underclass "academies" and slum yard bars (*piringundines*) of its origins, or the cabarets and "athletic or sports clubs" of its golden age, is still viewed askance by opinion-mongers who encourage standards and tastes that prove their ignorance of the dance floor, and a lethargic sensitivity. *Milongas* is not meant for these self-appointed disciples of Adorno.

This book means to cherry-pick its own readers: not necessarily milonga dancers, but certainly enthusiasts, people who can't help but feel moved as their eyes follow the spectacle of a soberly dressed older couple sashaying across the dance floor, unfussy, at three in the morning in some neighborhood dance hall, crossing in front of a younger couple, he in a pair of sneakers that could never "sand a shaving of wood from the dance floor," she in jeans, performing the most strenuous figures. The couples are not mutually exclusive. That they coincide in these same wee hours of a night, only a few meters away from each other, enraptured by the same music, is the height of glory.

E. C.,
August 2007

Ceremonies of the Present

Salón Canning: Transfiguration

It was Vivi Tellas who clarified for me why so many pretty young girls in the dance hall remained seated with their backs to the wall, wearing a sullen air only a few were able to disguise as indifference, watching as men summoned to dance older and plumper women who lacked any observable appeal.

"No doubt they dance with lead feet . . ."

That night in Salón Canning, while the DJ played one Fresedo track after another and not a single Pugliese, Don Samuel, at eighty years and counting, had no intention of letting a single tango slip him by. Dressed in his brown suit and shapeless hat of the same color, he led out to dance any fair-haired woman dramatically taller than him. I'd bought him a drink once and without calling attention to his stature, questioned his patent predilection; I think I said something along the lines of: So, I see you aren't afraid of

Scandinavians. He flashed me a big-hearted smile, as if transmitting a bit of know-how in life to the next generation.

"*Pibe*, nothing beats having your head lodged between a nice pair of tits."

I'd never seen him in Niño Bien or in Porteño y Bailarín. It occurs to me that he's never ventured beyond Villa Crespo, though my speculations might be an early glimmer, I feel it, in the process that leads to me turning him into a fictional character. But for the time being, I haven't yet framed the story for him to step into.

Who else could I use as a prototype for a fictional character? Aunt Nelly? I met her one Thursday at one in the morning, more or less, in Niño Bien, I was with Martín Maisonave and we couldn't find a free table. Candela suggested we share one, and that's how I saw this woman for the first time, so punctiliously clad and coiffed, who received us with a guarded smile. When Martín sat down and offered a courteous "with your permission, Ma'am," she corrected him on the fly: "It's Nelida, if you don't mind, though everyone calls me Aunt Nelly."

Like many traditional *milongueros*, Aunt Nelly prefers to dance to Canaro and D'Arienzo, orchestras that play sustained rhythms and tempos. Pugliese's music, she explained, is only for listening. It didn't seem an appropriate time to explain to her that Pugliese's *rubatos* are what most appeal to me when I'm dancing, those instants when the music seems to dangle on the brink of a lull, when the bandoneons briefly swoon before catching their breath again. It struck me to think how that confrontation with the telltale pause had never loomed above Aunt Nelly's milonga-dancing horizon. "Don't even think of uttering the name Típica Fernández Fierro to her," Martín whispered prudently.

Yet Don Samuel and Aunt Nelly are such rich characters in and of themselves that what little I've learned about them is already too much to allow my imagination to run freely and build a plot around them and their escapades. So what if I start from the other end of the equation?

I once heard someone say, I don't remember who: "Let me die on the dance floor, and let them sweep my body away so the dancing can go on . . ." Or might it have been something that occurred to me on one of those nights of wild abandon, my head riven by alcohol and countless reproaches we thought were filed away, "in these bleak hours / when even the stains on our suit / keep us company" (Jaime Gil de Biedma, "La novela de un joven pobre"). Who should I give it to?

There's an older, distinguished gentleman I've seen in Canning on several occasions. He's always dressed to the nines in an impeccable navy blue suit with light, barely visible pinstripes, a handkerchief as white as his shirt peeking from his breast pocket, folded crisply into three stern tips. Being bald hasn't discouraged him from allowing the gray hair around his temples and nape to flourish, which he has combed over creatively. Remarkably slender, he dances untiringly, in a style so classic as to shun the slightest sign of accent or ornament. His attention homes in effortlessly on the young women charmed by his attention, whose eyelids lower and lips part just slightly, into dreamy expressions. ("Never trust a woman who dances with open eyes," I heard my father say once.) Shall I choose him?

So let's say that one night he sees a girl he likes from among the pretty girls nobody is asking to dance. I eschew all banal psychological ploys: she doesn't remind him of some lost childhood sweetheart (cheap fiction), or his wife when she was still young and fresh (irredeemable reality), not even a daughter that went "missing" (ideological opportunism). He's simply partial to her. Very.

He smiles at her. She, a bit disbelieving perhaps, hesitates slightly before smiling back. He reinforces his tacit invitation with a nod. She doubts no longer. She stands up and steps forward self-assuredly, responding to his prompt. Not a word is spoken between them. He places his right arm around her waist, taking up her right hand in his left. His movements are at once gentle and firm. They stand interlocked and sway softly for two or three beats until he opens with his left foot and she follows like a shadow. No, like an extension of his body. No, like a response to his steps, because her feet dare accompany the austerity of his movements, always in a backwards gesture, with an aerial ornament. She's becoming something else now: in the arms of this distinguished milonga dancer, she acquires an unimagined air of poise, of suppleness. Thanks to him she's no longer just another pretty girl who can't dance. And his expression reveals another transformation: thanks to her, to holding the woman he clearly desires in his arms, the old fellow has become the irresistible ladies' man he probably never was in youth, in the dregs of what many people call "real life." For all of three minutes and twenty seconds, the fictional identity insinuated by this man, this woman, by the music and dance, has called into question and even banished the idea of marital status.

They remain stock-still in a figure when the music comes to an end, as if they had come upon it casually. Wouldn't it be the ideal moment for him to die? If only the end of life were like this, a mere interruption . . .

But no. That shocked expression on her face doesn't appeal to me, the panic, one hand raised to her mouth concealing a scream of silent horror. And I'd prefer not to picture the kindly young attendants retiring an inert body from the dance floor, or the flummoxed expressions of other couples, that uncertain moment of grief that never quite declares itself before the subsequent musical score allows for the dance, somewhat timorously, to recommence . . .

I'd prefer to leave this admirable older gentleman, whom I myself would like to resemble, holding the girl there in his arms, fixed in the perfection of that final figure of the tango they danced. The only death I offer him is the interruption of this story.

The Flaneur:
Roaming

Scattered over the face of the earth, [. . .]
differing in color and features, only one thing – the Secret –
unites them and will unite them until the end of time.
　　　　　Jorge Luis Borges, "The Sect of the Phoenix"

It's a biting, blustery Wednesday in November, and I venture out
in search of Café Stacja, at ten thirty in the evening, through the
dimly lit streets of Kazimiercz, Kraków's old quarters. Google has
promised me that on this day of the week there will be a milonga in
this café, starting at eleven p.m.

　　I get lost along the way and find myself in the center of what
remains of the Jewish neighborhood, it's anyone's guess whether it
has been restored, and if so to what extent: there's a small square
with a commemorative plaque, and skirting it is the synagogue,

the cemetery, the Klezmer Hotel, Aleph restaurant, and several welcoming winks at the prosperous North American tourist industry. Local agencies suggest following the path Spielberg took, who filmed certain sequences of *Schindler's List* in the vicinity, or making a pilgrimage ("a day trip") to Auschwitz, some eighty kilometers away. . . . I can't help but view this as a staged act of expiation that verges on the obscene. I walk away, quietly humming the tango "Buenos Aires, Queen of the River Plate . . ."

Eventually I locate Café Stacja. On first sight, nothing about the place stands out to me as particularly exotic: it could be any small neighborhood tavern in Munich or Prague. At one point the lights dim nearly imperceptibly, which deepens the darkness of the walls, a blend of dusky wood and rough-hewn stone. A DJ somewhere out of sight switches off the elevator music that was playing when I came in, and turning up the volume, the voice of Alberto Castillo resounds in "Así se baila el tango." And as if heeding the call of a *canyengue* version of the pied piper (*canyengue* points to a streetwise quality, a swaggering confidence that isn't disdainful but smilingly knowing of behavior that might not be decent), five or six couples move away from their tables to occupy an empty space in the center that I hadn't noticed (and would never have thought to call a dance floor) and begin performing the most spectacular figures, ones they could have picked up from Miguel Angel Zotto or Juan Carlos Copes.

Once the moment of confusion is over, I pay close attention to the show of skill and dexterity, though unadmiringly: I recognize something mechanical in the movements that had amazed me at first. Carlos Di Sarli's "El pollo Ricardo" comes on after Juan Pedro Castillo. Not far from me, there's a young girl with ivory skin and that flaxen hair many Polish women have, riveted by the dancers' steps. "A tango student," I tell myself, and encouraged by what I interpret as modesty, I approach her and pronounce the customary "Would you like to dance?" Colossal mistake. A few bars later and it's crystal clear. The alleged student "takes me down." In no time at all, it's me who is trying to follow her, a hardened milonga dancer, and I'm flabbergasted by her expertise. So I try a *sandwichito*, introducing my foot between hers, and in return she gives an unrequested hook; scarcely have I thought to flex my left leg when she instantly she counters with a tiny *sentadita*, or sitting figure. When the tango ends, I burble some excuse for my clumsiness and invite her to my table. She asks my nationality and I'm overwhelmed by a little swell of patriotism. In defense of the national honor I respond: "From Uruguay."

Poland and milonga, an unsuspected yet steadfast partner . . .

Four months later, one February night in London with the unfulfilled promise of snow in the air, I head over to Exhibition Road, South Kensington, to find a milonga. This venue is altogether different: held on the first floor of the Polish Hearth Club, whose restaurant I had been to the summer before. There are tables on a terrace outside, overlooking the private gardens of residents on a very exclusive city block.

I had never suspected that there, on the first floor, the so-called Milonga de la Luna was held every Saturday night. The dance floor is no smaller than the one at El Beso, on Riobamba Street in Buenos Aires, but the tables are arranged near the entrance and not in a circle, so it's hard to keep an eye on the dancers when they move towards the back of the salon. I pick out Hispanic accents among the crowd, though not from the Río de la Plata region; it also seems to me that some single ladies, smiling, eager, are British.

Next weekend is carnival, though I suspect it's not widely celebrated on these islands. The Milonga de la Luna is publicizing a special event on Saturday, when a fantasy session with a make-up artist comes with the price of entry: "Discover your true self!" In Buenos Aires, I think, nobody needs the help of cosmetics to affect an imaginary identity, it's assumed automatically with the music and dancing from the moment you step foot in a milonga.

The invisible DJ favors Florindo Sassone and Osvaldo Fresedo. The couples are reserved, competent, and free from the exhibitionism that had stunned me in Kraków. Still smarting over my little mishap in Café Stacja, I don't try to ask anyone to dance, but instead chitchat with the waitress on her breaks: she has no interest in dancing, but likes to listen to tango, and she talks about Piazzolla with the detached respect of a preordained religion; she's the daughter of Polish parents, born in England, and she's saving up for a trip to Argentina.

As I listen to her, I peruse the portraits along the walls of the Georgian mansion, seat of the Polish government in exile during the Second World War, of aristocratic ladies and decorated officers who had joined the British military. Patriots all, they were betrayed in Yalta when Churchill and Roosevelt handed half of Eastern Europe over to Stalin. It's as if they were observing the dancing with a kind of bemused skepticism.

—

I admit being drawn to the victims of History, or perhaps it's better to say the defeated; though I don't care at all for the darker side of things, the kinky, which is an acquired taste that seems over-cultivated to me. This explains why it took me such a long time to check in on another London milonga, despite its evocative sounding name: El Once, Eleven. The location is what put me off at first: the crypt of a church, Saint James's Crypt on the Green, in Islington.

I finally plucked up the nerve one Saturday to travel by tube to Farringdon Station and emerged there onto a distinctly refurbished neighborhood, far from the elegant 17th century suburb where Cromwell had resided, and from its years of decadence after World War Two and the slow eclipse of the Industrial Revolution. I have a beer in The Crown Tavern and read on a plaque that in 1903, the pub was called The Crown and Anchor, and frequented by the young Stalin and Lenin, being only a few blocks from where the *Iskra* newspaper was published. I walk by number 37 on Clerkenwell Green and another plaque tells me it's home to the Marx Memorial Library. I also pass by several restaurants with minimalist decor and spotlights pointing to signs announcing *cuisine d'auteur* or *cuisine du marché*, and a little farther along, a Dolce & Gabbana boutique and a nightclub called Potemkin.

Michiko Okazaki and Paul Lange greet me at The Crypt, veteran hosts accustomed to welcoming random guests. They founded El Once, they tell me, thirteen years earlier and moved just a few years ago into what everyone calls The Crypt, but without the macabre air; it's where they celebrate the "saturnal" milongas. Classes are held on Monday. And truly, the brick and stone vaults don't strike me as a proper backdrop for Bram Stoker, maybe on account of the young couples sashaying across the parquet dance floor, a traditional requisite of any milonga, to the drilling, untraditional rhythm of Gotán Project's latest CD. When I clarified that electronic tango is not my shot of vodka, Paul remained impervious: "We play some 'less frequented' sounds, too. Juan Maglio?"

It's my experience that the more romantic the setting for a milonga, the worse the dancers. Every summer, more or less between June and September, Paris allows different groups to organize dances along the quays of the Seine in the fifth arrondissement, by the

Institut du Monde Arabe. Fashioned as a promenade with gardened commons, this area, the lower quays, plays host on summer nights to African music, salsa dancing, and tango, filling the diverse nooks and crannies along the river with people. The sound system is humble: a CD player with speakers that amplify and deform the music. Yet the enthusiasm of natives and tourists alike is unmistakable and even unfaltering despite the sporadic presence of police who come to sniff the air in pursuit of herbaceous perfumes wafting into the nocturnal breeze. Many of the dancers are dressed in sneakers or sandals, and don't do much more than sway to the music that sounds so exotic to them; a few in the know negotiate a bit of space over the quay's hard cobblestone, a surface that is perfectly contrary to the smooth parquet floors required by tango. The get-togethers kick off at around ten in the evening, and the June sky stays light until after midnight.

From time to time a sightseeing boat crosses the landscape: it offers a radiant spectacle, reflectors illuminating the shore, revealing the phantasmagoria of the most austere façades, bestowing the dancers with a fleeting stage presence.

I've never actually been in the loft just above the wholesale butcher shop Two Flags Butcher Supply Co. in New York City. It's in the old neighborhood in downtown Manhattan called the Meatpacking

District, beside the Hudson River. In the years before AIDS, the area was renowned as a market for non-edible meat. SM buffs used to take part in group ceremonies in freezer trucks parked in front of the wharf, and drag queens would hazard to cross the cobbled Belgian-block roads in twelve-inch heels.

New York's tradition of perpetual transformation has turned that loft into a milonga. The manager, Carina Möller, is from Berlin, she studied modern dance in her hometown before landing in New York in the mid-90s with a collection of 300 tango CDs. Same as in Buenos Aires, the evening begins with classes before moving on to the milonga proper. Möller follows classic criteria in her teaching: "The basic element of tango is the walk, and it's not up for debate," she asserts categorically.

I've never been to Moscow during the northern hemisphere's summer solstice, the days on either side of June 21st, the longest of the year, when they celebrate the Milonguero Nights. I receive their email every year: Sasha, by first name only, announces a cast of Argentine professors who will guide the neophytes, and he recommends affordable lodging in the capital that is now, in modern times, one of the most expensive cities on the planet. It's their fifth year and they've changed the dates in 2007 to August, to better accommodate European tourism. Sasha proudly informs me that Los Cosos de al Lao will be performing this year. I remember (I imagine with the nostalgia of what I've never experienced) the promise they made that first year: the closing event will be held outdoors, in Red Square, between the Kremlin and St. Basil's Cathedral.

On certain evenings in Buenos Aires when I watch Asians dance (people who come from what, in this extreme West, we call the East), abandoning themselves to the music in a way that reminds me of the tango cult in Japan, I remember my father, a seaman, who would have learned to dance tango in 1940, before he set sail on the training vessel Argentina: the ship's final destination was Yokohama and the officers were expected to represent the country in a dignified manner. . . . The host country received the crew with full honors. My father told me stories about the reception in Osaka where he danced two or three tangos with very elegant, silent ladies dressed in kimonos; he was never sure whether they were geishas or the wives of ministers.

Nor am I familiar with the milongas in Oslo or Ulan Bator. I'm sure, however, that were I to visit these cities one day, I'd search them out. My innocent, leisurely research has become my private passion and by aligning it with my travels, I'm able to enrich my collection without it ever taking me over completely.

What I won't find, I'm afraid, is what in my own city can stir me so deeply: that random, tentative after-hour neighborhood locale where an elderly couple not yet ready for bed slips out for a last saunter around the dance floor – not necessarily their last – and the indefatigable young couple who stops to watch them attentively, with the respect they deserve as living examples of a tradition that is being lost, while the staff busy themselves arranging the chairs on top of the tables, serenely, making time as the closing hour approaches, careful not to get in the way of the last dancers or make them feel unwelcome. And that's when I sense there's time left for one last glass of champagne. Not necessarily the last.

Music From a Lost Time:
Necromancy

On the early side of the 21st century, the gay milonga in Buenos Aires, La Marshall, attracted an admirably mixed crowd that gave no hint of being a marginal ghetto, and couples danced to "Otoño porteño," "Prepárense," even "Oblivion." Now that La Marshall is extinct, the Queer Tango festivals have taken its place.

The music at La Marshall bestowed these couples with a nearly immaterial lightness. Gliding across the dance floor in measured yet robust movements, careful to keep a certain distance between their bodies, the dancers took visible pleasure in using improvised choreographies fusing classical tango figures with unexpected new forms. It wasn't the milonguero style of tango with contact between cheeks and chests; neither did it have the air of ballroom tango; every once in a while you'd catch a slight acrobatic movement characteristic of the so-called "tango spectacle." And yet the couples reached the same trance-like state that so elates dancers in more traditional milongas.

When asked twenty years earlier, "Why is tango ever less popular as a dance?" Piazzolla responded categorically, "It's not something I worry about because I don't play music for dancing. I play tango for listening, so it's not my problem." I wonder what he might have thought about watching such a "spectacle."

———

There's a night that's gone down in milonga history, a night historical for the tango, too. And like any historical event, at the time it seemed like just another episode in the daily life of the people who experienced it.

It took place in the early 40s, during the carnival festivities at Boca Junior's sports club. At one point that evening, Aníbal Troilo, better known as Pichuco, led his orchestra in an arrangement of "Inspiración," put together by their young bandoneonist, Astor Piazzola. Several people stopped dancing and left the floor. Others drew nearer to the musicians, wanting to pay closer attention.

That was the virtual debutant's moment of illumination: his music would become a version of tango meant for listening. Legend has it that afterwards Pichuco entreated Dedé, Piazzolla's first wife: "Please get him to stop, he's going to turn my orchestra into a symphony . . ." Over the years, earning his independence at a steep price, exploring his early intuitions more deeply, Piazzolla would go on to distill an essence of tango: a form at once familiar and yet resurrected into a new life.

—

According to Gidon Kremer, what makes Piazzolla's music so unique among his contemporaries is how it ignores outright the boundaries between "cultivated" and "popular" forms of music. At once sentimental and yet also sophisticated, the work of a clearly refined musician who instead of compiling "music for composers," chose to stir deep emotion in the most wide-ranging audiences, Piazzolla went on to carve out a category of his own at the second half of the 20th century.

Kremer's insight, however, doesn't dispel the mystery of how an ever-expanding series of concentric circles went on to conquer new territories and soloists, since Piazzolla himself recorded *Five Tango Sensations* with the Kronos Quartet just a few months before his death, in 1991. Kremer was a Lithuanian violinist who created the Astor Quartet to interpret Piazzolla's music roughly three decades ago. He continued his work with another ensemble, "Kremerata Baltica," for which he assembled musicians from the Baltic and Scandinavian countries to play with the soloists of his original quartet: the Norwegian bandoneonist Per-Arne Glorvigen, the Russian pianist Vadim Sakharov, and the Austrian double bassist Alois Posch. Kremer titled his first recording in homage to Piazzolla

Le Grand Tango, which was arranged by Sofia Gubaidulina, the Russian composer censored during Soviet times because her work allegedly bore the influence of Anton Webern. Though Kremer's tribute is the most structured and original, he wasn't alone: Yo-Yo Ma, Daniel Barenboim, and Emmanuel Ax are other classically trained musicians who have recorded Piazzolla's compositions.

The Argentine composer able to inspire such fervent devotion among musicians so far removed from his own origins and tradition is certainly an unparalleled case in contemporary music. Each of the testimonies of those who knew him describe him as having a difficult character, as is the case with all creators convinced of the value of something they wish to impose on a public that's not yet prepared for it. But he was also typically Argentine, prey to alternating raptures of love and resentment for his country, emotions perfectly familiar to his fellow nationals – but perhaps more extreme in his case – Piazzolla felt that Argentina fought against him and cajoled him by turns, and in the end figured it had won him over.

There's an image of the composer as a child, unforgettable for anyone: he's playing the role of newspaper hawker, wearing a cap on his head and carrying a bundle of papers under his arm, right hand pointing to something beyond the frame for a group of men; among them is Carlos Gardel, dressed in a canotier hat, a white wing-collar shirt and broad tie, and beside him is Tito Luisardo, and an extra in police garb. The scene is from *El día que me quieras*, the crooner's penultimate movie, which was filmed in Paramount's Long Island studios in early 1935, the year of his death . . .

Piazzolla's childhood on New York's Lower East Side and adolescence in Buenos Aires, between musical arrangements for Troilo and classes with Ginastera, led him to spend a decisive year in Paris, between 1954 and 1955, where his composition teacher, the legendary Nadia Boulanger, encouraged him to plumb his true roots for inspiration in tango. From that moment on, Piazzolla's journey reads like a sequence of exiles and homecomings, between hard-liner manifestos (the "decalogue" when putting together the Buenos Aires Octet) and acceptance of his role as a dissident (with the Nuevo Tango Quintet), his offhand remarks and misunderstandings with colleagues or self-proclaimed tango "academics." It also describes an uncompromising engagement with his very personal view of music and the path he'd chosen to blaze.

—

Borges used to quote an intuition of Oscar Wilde's he found particularly insightful: "music reveals to us an unknown and perhaps real past" (*Other Inquisitions*). He developed the notion in one of his later poems ("El tango"): "The tango creates a murky, unreal past / that somehow becomes true, / an impossible memory . . ."

To him, that past was a saga of *guapos* and dagger fights in a slum at once neighboring yet forbidden, something dreamt before actually glimpsed beyond the iron rails that separated the sensible space of the yard from the dangerous street outside, a space that the boy who found refuge in a "library of nearly infinite English books" in his paternal home in Palermo, both feared and desired. That universe, already defunct in 1930 when Borges conjures it back in *Evaristo Carriego*, was still dormant in the 60s, when he tries to resuscitate it again in lyrics for milongas and poems.

One individual's lost time is different from anyone else's, and yet the feelings of loss over something beloved, the utter betrayal of time, is common to all human beings. The past that was restored to Borges through tango belongs to him alone, and probably matters very little to his readers, but towards the end of the 20th century that same music (the poet preferred milonga, the dance, to the song, free of the Italianizing influence he so detested) seemed to reinstate something beloved, something lost, to ever more listeners.

Piazzolla's introspective, brooding music, where even the danceable cadences are channeled by way of fugues and counterpoints that never relinquish emotional potency and the richness of melody, is to me the antithesis of Borges's shortsighted prejudices, and splendidly Italianizing from within the melting pot that is the Río de la Plata region. His music has become the vehicle for so many people in search of their own particular lost time: the Russian, the Japanese, the Lithuanian, they've all acknowledged something familiar in it, something lived, secretly, and lost forever. It's the kind of music one listens to in solitude, even in the midst of a multitude. The way the unorthodox duos in La Marshall danced, alone, even in the midst of a crowded dance floor.

—

What impressed me the most about these couples was how estranged they were from their surroundings, in a sort of visible, sensory self-absorption: I see the same thing in the conjoined bodies sashaying across the dance floor of the most traditional milongas. The music possesses them and they submit to it in a state of hypnotic abandon, where Martínez Estrada identifies the descent of the soul into the body, its animation made manifest through the dance.

Piazzolla has been the great demiurge, maybe even the first of this tacit necromancy. His music possesses, yes, but it doesn't bewilder these dancers whom he'd never anticipated: he demands skill and exactitude. By salvaging for dance a music not composed for it, by appropriating it, the bygone partners are reincarnated in these young bodies, characters unknown to them, the dead fleetingly come back to life to perform movements suggested to them by music they were never able to hear themselves. I feel as though I recognize the same couples who charmed a travel writer nearly a century ago: "The dancing I see tonight in this dive in Buenos Aires is the embodiment of training, self-control, wise application, and refined artifice."

At this hour of the night the milonga, all milongas, even the ones so far-removed from Piazzolla's music, become "A region where Yesterday could / Be Today, and Still and Yet" (Borges).

And not only by night. The day my mother turned ninety-five, on the threshold of Alzheimer's Palace, I asked where she would like to go. It didn't take her long to answer: "I want to see tango dancing." I took her to El Arranque, an early evening milonga where older couples, even elderly ones, are in the majority. Her slow entrance, prudent, reinforced by a cane and my arm, her empty gaze, her age highlighted by the make-up that was meant to cover it up, didn't go unnoticed. Fêted with champagne by Juan Carlos Lafalce, the organizer, she spent a speechless hour and a half there, graced with a vague smile, and I imagine transported to one of those Saturday afternoons when she was sixteen and used to dance at a friend's house, whose parents had scrupulously selected the masculine guests.

At a certain point, one of the scarce younger couples approached respectfully. The girl asked:

"Is she the lady Carmencita Calderón?"

I didn't dare divulge the fact in front of my mother that just a few weeks earlier, El Cachafaz's legendary partner had passed away at one hundred years of age; but before I could correct the mix-up, my mother, still smiling, countered:

"Not any longer."

Nameless Milonga:
Resurrection

The two of us will live the quarter hour
of nostalgic and wicked dancing.
Pleasure of the Gods, perverse
dance, tango is rite and religion.

Frollo & Randle, *Danza maligna*

I'd been watching her for a while. Openly at first, not bothering to hide my fascination with that face that seemed designed by a scalpel; later furtively: I started to worry that my staring might make her feel uncomfortable, though she didn't seem to notice at all.

When she was invited out to dance, though, I felt free to admire her tall, willowy figure without hiding, the aloof elegance of her movements, how she held her head high above her slender neck now concealed, now revealed by her ash-blond hair as she swayed to the rhythm of the music. But it was her face, barely amended by cosmetics, that attracted my scrutiny. The artificial brushed up against the monstrous in her features, bestowing an unimagined *bellezza medusea*, the Italian art historian Mario Praz's notion of hypnotic beauty: deep-set eyes, as if they'd been unsealed in a skin they hadn't been born to; overly chiseled cheekbones and eyebrows that seemed carved from intractable materials; plump, meaty lips devoid of the sensuality oft-pledged by aesthetic surgery.

I watched her nurse her champagne in slow sips. She conceded little attention to the people around her. There was a young girl by her side at all times, plain-featured and with a timid smile, blessed with no saving graces, no hint of the mystery and charm that can make a woman who isn't beautiful, attractive. It brought to mind – a longstanding reader of James never sleeps – "The Beldonald Holbein," the story of Lady Beldonald, a mature beauty who thinks herself clever by calling on the company of a prune-faced old woman, touched by hardship, to enhance by comparison her withering charms. Her artist friends become fascinated by this face that seems straight from a Holbein painting, and only have eyes for her. Lady Beldonald learns the lesson: for the next season in London, she'll appear in society with a plain young girl, not even ugly, by her side.

Could the object of my curiosity have come to a similar conclusion?

One night we were seated at neighboring tables. I thought I knew how to camouflage my curiosity, but at some point she surprised me with her eyes fixed from amidst the surgical feat of her face, which was framed by straight, unbound hair. It didn't seem to bother her; quite the contrary, she sketched out a smile.

"You recognize me, don't you?"

Puzzled, caught off guard in my indiscretion, I heard leap from the tip of my tongue an opportune riposte.

"Yes, but how could I ever dare think it was really you."

The smile declared itself and I felt I should ask her to dance. I think the DJ had chosen Fresedo's "Vida mía." She was incredibly light in my arms, and resolved effortlessly and without reproach the inevitable uncertainty of my self-conscious moves. The tango series came to an end and we returned to our tables. Just then, a man greeted her. His intrusion allowed me to sneak away.

I ran into El Turco at the door, restless jaw below a toothless mouth, Hawaiian shirt and his scant strands of hair tied back with a tiny rubber band. I asked about my mysterious dance partner.

"What do you mean? You don't remember her?"

He summarized the fleeting and not very illustrious career of Natalia Franz, a "kitten" who for a variety of reasons had been disrobed and hounded by ageing or obese comics in the theater of magazine shows and so-called comedy programs on television. It seems she wasn't meant for better or brighter triumphs, when she was disfigured in a motorcycle accident. Eight operations in the space of two years produced the miracle that had prompted my attention: a face that was the product of design, not organic life, where only a twinkle in those sunken yet alert eyes revealed the presence of a living creature behind the fused and frozen mask.

I was obliged to buy a gram from El Turco in exchange for his information. I escorted him to the "gentlemen's" to better conceal a transaction that, it was common knowledge, was his only reason for being at the milonga. Between the standard and what he called the "gold," I opted for the first, which was half the price of the second; the poor quality of what El Turco distributed didn't warrant extravagances, and anyway, it'd been a few years since I'd tried it. Once outside, I slipped the powdery "papelito" to the man watching over the cars, knowing that he'd most likely resell it.

A few days later I told my story to Flavia Costa.

"It has to be someone else. I remember Franz. She died on the operating table a few years ago. She couldn't take the anesthesia."

The next time I saw her she was dancing with a man of undefined age, his toupee arranged atop what remained of his own hair, dyed that tone of black that looks so glossy and well-irrigated that it could never have sprouted from such withery and weathered skin. The same coquettish convention I accept with women has always seemed pathetic to me when it comes to men: clearly the reverberation of an archaic brand of sexism. Or rather, pathetic in men of a certain age, where the guiding purpose is to conceal their years on earth; I get a kick out of the motley locks of hair dyed synthetic colors in young men, the metallic piercings in ears and cheekbones.

Seeing this old man in camouflage drew my attention to an aspect of the public I hadn't noticed until then. Most of the women were heavily made-up, their faces plastered into colored crusts, hair frozen in hieratic constructions or seared into a shock of tight curls. They looked almost like drag queens with their surfeit of outwardly feminine virtues, which bestowed, as one can imagine, not the slightest hint of youth. A robust number of men extended the use of hair dye to include eyebrows and moustache, forsaking their skin to a tone of mortuary pallor. It reminded me of how a funeral parlor prepares a cadaver for viewing in the U.S., painting a veneer that instead of simulating a blissful sleep looks more like the impervious expression of a wax museum figure. Natalia Franz's operations are in another orbit compared to these faces, I told myself: a brutal fraud, yet nevertheless virtually ascetic. Her features attracted my gaze, obviously morbid, while these other creatures made me avert my eyes immediately, in any direction.

Funeral parlor . . . I think it was the instant these words came to me that I was overcome by a vague sense of dread. I stepped outside, where a few of the venerable couples were smoking cigarettes. Bereft now of the flattering lights in the milonga, the gaucherie of their overelaborate masks was accentuated by the street lamps. One of the women smiled without parting her lips, like someone trying to obscure dental pandemonium; perhaps, like El Turco, she'd lost faith in the virtue of prosthetics. I strode away without looking back, turned the corner at Acevedo and onto Córdoba.

At the time, I was developing an idea for a screenplay, suggested to me by a film director friend. The Chinese, he told me, don't want to die outside of their homeland; if they do, their souls will never be at rest. So a group of elderly Chinese, feeling the end of days nigh, pools their humble savings to charter a boat to carry them to San Francisco, Canton, or Taipei. (The ship . . . a romantic idea, anachronistic. Nowadays, wouldn't it be easier to charter a plane? Isn't San Francisco a little dubious with its over-hyped Chinatown? Why not Lima?) But the captain and crew swindle them and abandon them in some port city, maybe Honolulu. Once the trickery is manifest, the resulting angst is too much for the old folks and some of them die. One young sailor, not in cahoots with his superiors, rises to the task of deliverance and manages to provide handfuls of symbolic Chinese earth heaved from the consular garden, on which to rest their heads when they feel the end approaching.

The idea appealed to me, just like how all things irrational appeal to me, how they guide human behavior, but I couldn't see a way for that ending to work visually, it seemed good for a story but problematic for the screen. I considered suggesting to my director friend a story unrelated to China: a story about some elderly dancers who after death are given the gift of an eternal milonga, where they would endure forever, blissful, consecrated to the rites they observed in life. Later I realized that if my observations at Villa Crespo hadn't been the spark for the idea, they had certainly fed into it. The story's twist comes at the end, when the observer, thinking he has come to the milonga by chance, realizes that in fact he's dead, too. My friend wasn't convinced.

"So that's the best you can do in the morbid category?"

Whatever the case, Natalia Franz was alive. The day after we danced, her delicate, floral scent continued to linger on my right cheek. I wondered what she'd look like in the daylight, outside the tiny milonga with its soft, honey-colored lighting. Maybe she avoided exposure to the sun ... though the sun had remained hidden behind more or less dogged clouds for an entire week. Where does she live? Her name, likely a pseudonym, wasn't listed in the phone book. These leisurely questions kept me entertained, distracted, while I neglected my pursuit of a novel-worthy, visually arresting denouement for my friend's movie idea.

I returned to the Villa Crespo milonga one night, half-heartedly, not very confident I'd catch sight of her forged face again. I thought I could recognize the same cast of characters, or maybe another troupe of them indistinguishable from the original one. I stood at the bar and watched the dancers for a while. The DJ beside me had no use for the modern perks of a laptop like the one I'd seen Boggio using at Canning; he hadn't even evolved yet to using tapes or CDs: in a show of astonishing skill, he alternated LP records between two separate turntables.

My quest to find Natalia Franz had proven unsuccessful. I was heading towards the door, feeling defeated, when there in a shadowy nook I recognized her, alongside her habitual, nearly invisible companion. I hadn't seen her come in and could have sworn that when my gaze passed over the table just a split second earlier, it had been empty. I chose a straightforward approach.

"After we danced last week, your perfume lingered several days. I couldn't help but be reminded of you. It's a floral scent . . . but which flower?"

She snickered under her breath.

"My friends call me Tuberose on account of that perfume."

We danced to Pichuco's "La bordona." On guard not to stumble into other couples on the tiny dance floor, at one point I caught a glimpse of our reflection in a mirror. I recognized Natalia Franz, or the woman I thought was her, but the man she was dancing with seemed like a caricature of the one I assumed was me. How could I possibly have aged so much that my less-than-elegant figure – I *was* aware – had become so graceless? I looked away and saw what seemed like the hint of a conspiratorial and slightly teasing smile from the table in the shadowy nook that seemed to imagine what I was feeling. It was Natalia's young companion.

I can't remember the excuse I used to quit that milonga, but I put some distance between Villa Crespo and myself. I called Flavia on my cell and once again filled her in on what had happened.

"Better watch yourself, you could fall prey to your own fiction.

I'll get dressed and we can meet up. It's Thursday, let's meet at Niño Bien."

I waited for her at the door of the Lion's Club on Humberto Primo Street, whose first floor livens up every Thursday with one of my favorite milongas. Before Flavia showed up and rescued me from my own fiction, I told myself it would be best to consider my days as a flaneur over. I'm too old to be spellbound by ghosts and their secrets. From now on I'll practice restraint, only attend my favorite milongas, dance with friends, and forget all the treacherous mysteries and bad literature lurking round the poorly lit streets and minuscule dance floors. If they wanted to tell me something, I'd prefer to be kept in the dark as long as possible.

That night Flavia and I closed the place.

Taking Minutes of Bygone Times

Anno Mirabilis *1913*

1913, the year of tango, in light of subsequent
events [. . .] the silliest year in world history.

H. G. Wells

In a tango tournament in Paris, in 1913, a couple was awarded a prize after dancing seventy-two tangos straight without collapsing. In the late November issue of that same year's *Il Teatro Illustrato*, we're told, "They're dancing tango all over Italy." The date and time of the first tango danced in the Finnish capital of Helsinki was recorded: November 2, 1913; on stage at the Apollo Theater, Southern Esplanade, at two in the afternoon. That November, tango was also danced for the first time in Warsaw: it was a special skit inside an American operetta at the Teatr Nowości. The Parisian writer and caricaturist Sem (Georges Goursat) published an album called *Tangoville* in 1913, in which he caricatures Gabriele D'Annunzio and Ida Rubinstein dancing a tango: their figures appear in the steam given off by a plate of spaghetti. I discovered it in a volume rich in revelations titled *El tango nómade: ensayos sobre la diaspora del tango*, compiled by Ramón Pelinski. Though the reader must curb his or her enthusiasm over certain infelicities in the translation from the French to the Spanish. And caution grows when in a single paragraph we read that *Le Chien andalou*, Buñuel and Dali's film, débuted in Paris in 1920 (it was filmed in 1928) and that "later" Irene and Vernon Castle would bring tango to the United States . . . Not only did Vernon Castle crash his plane at the end of World War I, the famous ballroom dancing duo had already begun dancing it in 1914, performing for the Grand Duchess Anastasia, Tsar Nicolas II's sister, and that same year they inaugurated Castle House, the school through which they introduced the dance to the social elite of Manhattan, while publishing their manual, *Modern Dancing*.

La fièvre du tango, the tango craze . . . "Everyone danced the tango in 1913, one way or another. Mothers kept a wary eye on their daughters taking classes in the Baraduc dance school where Mr. Washington Lopp taught a *comme il faut* version of the new rhythm" (Julien Green, *Memories of Happy Days*). The Franco-American writer's sister, Retta, purchased an album with her own pocket money, on whose cover a heavy-lidded gaucho with opulent lips promised some form of ecstasy. Very soon Retta was playing a tango for her mother titled "Dans tes bras," whose tin ear precluded her from differentiating between this voluptuous melody and the

Muzio Clementi exercises given by a teacher named Madame de las Palmas.

Any occasion was ripe for tango dancing. The Parisian magazine *Fémina* published a humorous cartoon of a couple on the 1st of August, 1913. She is sporting an ankle-length coat and tightly-fitted hat that covers her hair, he a broad overcoat, leather cap and specs – they're decked out in the kind of protective gear worn by early motorists. They are dancing a tango outdoors, near a convertible stopped at the side of the road where a mechanic is trying to fill a flat tire, and a maid is turning the handle of a gramophone. The title of the cartoon is: *Pendant la panne* (During the Breakdown).

Tango took Europe by storm. A headline of *Argos* magazine in Saint Petersburg acknowledged: "Everyone is dancing the tango." The tango dress was not all that was trumpeted in cosmopolitan Prague, prior to the Soviet asphyxia, but also the tango corset, and a Czech composer debuted a stage operetta titled *Madame Tango*. At a time when a plethora of new rhythms were vying for audiences (the Brasilian *maxixa* was never popular enough to endure and even less so the European bear dance or turkey trot), the tango was able to last beyond a single season. It first became fashionable in Paris and spread out from there. When did it arrive? One could already read in *El Hogar* in Buenos Aires, on December 20, 1911, "the aristocratic ballrooms of the great capital city [Paris] unreservedly host a dance whose vile tradition precludes its name from even being pronounced in local salons."

The discrepancies that exist among testimonies only encourage me further. Oral lore says that President Raymond Poincaré and his wife danced a tango at the Institut d'Agronomie on April 1, 1913; according to *L'Osservatore Romano* (January 11, 1914), the same president ordered the orchestra at a reception in the Palais de l'Elysée to abstain from including any tango in its repertoire. An inconsistency? A reasonable distinction between two different public occasions, two different settings, perhaps? I've always been wary of certainties universally held: a nice cluster of uncertainties, on the other hand, only serves to rouse my curiosity, set me in motion. It's thanks to them that "Parisian tango," *locus classicus* of *porteño* legend, is getting lost in that misty zone where history slowly but surely slips into myth.

Sem alleges that 1912 was the "memorable year that saw the Argentine tango descend on Paris and venture its first challenging steps." Yet Alfredo Gobbi and Angel Villoldo had already arrived in 1907, sent by the Gath & Chaves label to record their first tangos on gramophones, and Gobbi founded a publishing imprint for his musical scores. And the poet André Salmon was sure he had seen a photograph of Ricardo Rojas and the self-proclaimed Vizconde de Lascano Tegui and other compatriots at Le Chat Blanc, a venue on Rue d'Odessa, "souvenir of the June night in 1908, where the first tango was danced in Montparnasse."

A hypothesis worthy of consideration suggests that tango required the flood of milonga dancers from elite families of apparently limitless resources, to make its way into the worldly ballrooms of Paris. Güiraldes, Madero, Videla Dorna all swept through the class of venues where Gobbi and Villoldo could take but a few tentative first steps. In their enterprise, these "niños bien" sanctified the orchestras of Pizzaro and Espósito.

In 1912, Max Linder's three-act film debuted, *Max professeur de tango* (or *Max als Tangolehrer*, since the French production was filmed in Berlin). The most original and popular comic actor of the time in Europe, whose films didn't go unnoticed by Chaplin, is mistaken by a group of prominent citizens for the tango instructor they were waiting for; to keep from exposing the error, Max has to come up with convincing dance steps, allowing him to flirt with one of the young heiresses.

In 1913, impostors pretending to be Argentine instructors began showing up to teach tango to wealthy women. One society writer poked fun at the situation: "*Dans tout Paris on se m'arrache! / De la vierge à la virago / chacune de moi s'amourache. / Je suis professeur de tango!*" ("In Paris everyone fights over me / from virgin to virago / head over heels you see / for I'm a teacher of tango!") Other more ambitious impostors passed themselves off as Russian or Italian nobles: "The police have discovered that these phony aristocrats take advantage of the complex postures required by tango to empty pockets and burgle jewelry." A year later, the legendary Irene and Vernon Castle advise enthusiasts in New York: "If feasible, take your classes with someone who has danced professionally in Paris:

there are so many good dancers in Paris that anyone who has danced there (and been paid for it) must necessarily be a good dancer." The comment on remuneration is not casual: Bernabé Simara was paid twelve hundred francs a month to teach two hours of tango a day at the Académie Rhynal and between thirty and forty to liven up the evenings of dancing in a fashionable restaurant. Alfredo, a character in Valentín de Pedro's novel for the stage, *El veneno del tango* (1927), tries to convince his girlfriend: "It's big business . . . I earn more in one night dancing tango in any old cabaret in Paris than in a month here at Don Luigi's department store."

Max Linder wasn't alone in creating a character whose humorous adventures and misadventures led to a series of short films. The tango craze inspired many of them. In England in 1914, the actor Sam Poluski, creator of the Nobby character, filmed *Nobby's Tango Teas*. The comedian Raymond Frau creator of the Kri Kri character, acted in an Italian film titled *Kri Kri e il tango*, and that same year Max Mack directed a German feature film, *Die Tango-Königin* (*The Tango Queen*). Nothing's known of several American films from 1914 that have the word tango in the title: *Tango versus Poker*, *A Tango Tragedy* (where apparently Oliver Hardy acts prior to working with Stan Laurel), and *Tango in Tuckerville*.

Its popularity was neither immediate nor unanimous. The gradual leveling out of tango's steps and figures to make it more palatable for European ballrooms (and by extension the "upper crust" families in Buenos Aires), together with the keen appetite of

Paris's cult of fashion, eager for even fleeting novelties, both helped consolidate the trend, flying in the face of polite society and even ecclesiastical disapproval. In 1914, Monseigneur Amette, the Archbishop of Paris, had to pay 20,000 francs for "pain and suffering" to an instructor named Stilson, who claimed his professional interests had been injured by the cleric when he banned tango from the pages of *La Semaine réligieuse*.

Jean Richepin (1849–1926), a versatile writer who was inducted into the Académie Française in 1908, had gained early notoriety for his poem cycle in *La Chanson des gueux*, whose picturesque misery hastily led to associations with Villon. Sporadic lover of Sarah Bernhardt, the diva encouraged him to venture into theater as an author and an actor. Keenly sensitive to public tastes long before the word marketing was ever coined, he debuted at the Théâtre de l'Athenée on December 30, 1913, with a comedy in four acts written together with his wife, titled *Le tango*. He had given a conference at the Institut de France ("*A propos du tango*") two months earlier, on October 25th, during the annual gathering of the five academies: the occasion, extensively commented on by journalists given the extraordinary, even scandalous, nature of the topic, could be seen as a publicity stunt for his comedy's upcoming debut.

The work itself was tailored to the tastes of a particularly Parisian audience, with a cortege of duchesses, princes, countesses, and other aristocrats entering and exiting the stage in a wide array of outfits, encouraging the pens of the most illustrious journalists.

The intrigue comes down to a sentimental imbroglio around a young aristocratic couple who are tango enthusiasts, and its resolution is a "great finale with the entire cast on stage," announced by the exclamatory sentence spoken by the young wife: "*Que c'est beau le tango!*". The audience received the multitudinous tango with wild applause on opening night, and praised the popular actress Eve Lavallière's cross-dressed portrayal of Prince Segismundo, nicknamed Zigi.

Even more remarkable is the patriotic delirium of Richepin's academic speech, which he used to promote his play, a writer whose career in public life was launched from the most unimpeachable left-wing trenches. The origins of tango, "born in abject pigsties," would be redeemed by the Greco-Latin spirit of France, legitimate heir of the classical virtues. One can just imagine the orator drawing from his brief experience on stage to rouse his audience's passion with the last three words of his speech: "*Patrie! Patrie! Patrie!*" Memory of the defeat of 1879 was still fresh in the minds of the elderly academics: months later, the First World War would become the occasion to arouse this senile frenzy outside the Institut de France.

Paris found meaning in the dance, beyond the pleasure of watching sensuousness barely veiled by choreography: "*Le tango c'est toujours un homme en face d'une femme qu'il désire. Le mécanisme des pas n'est plus apparent. C'est une improvisation à deux sur le rythme de l'orchestre, c'est l'univers réduit à un couple.*" ("Tango is always a man facing a woman he desires. The mechanism of steps doesn't matter. It's an improvisation for two, over the orchestral rhythm. It's the universe reduced to a couple!")

Unfaithful Memories

Each one of our lives is woven
with other lives.

E. C., *El rufián moldavo*

Scantily documented for decades, tango historians have had to rely on surviving players as a source, whose memories, as the years inevitably pass, dither, adorn, and omit. Each new testimony, new piece of information I find, seems to open endless new questions instead of bringing closure. And to me, the first impulse of fiction is to question experience, and memory, and to record. "Only connect," Forster said; "Only ask" would be my motto.

El Garrón, the cabaret on rue Fontaine number 6 bis, where they danced tango and would serve a hen stew in the wee hours, must have been the idea of Carlos's younger brother, Alberto López Buchardo (1882–1918). That's where the legendary Baron Megata

(1896–1968) learned tango. Tsunayoshi Megata, a.k.a. "Tsunami," son of a diplomat and grandson of a samurai, lived in Paris between 1920 and 1926. On his return to Tokyo, he became notorious for being the only one who danced authentic Argentine tango, and so he published a manual on the subject and founded an academy to teach the dance to the Japanese aristocracy. Doctor Luis Alfredo Aposta paid him homage in 1981 with the tango *A lo Megata*, whose music was arranged by Edmundo Rivero: "*Y así llevó el tango / a tierra nipona, / donde gratarola / lo enseñó a bailar. / Cuentan que Megata / no cobraba un mango, / por amor al tango / y por ser bacán.*" And so he brought tango / to Japanese lands / where free of charge / he taught them to dance. / They say Megata / charged not a mango, / for love of the tango / or to be high-falutin'.

The eldest of the López Buchardo family, a cultivated musician, had committed a single "youthful sin": he published the tango "Pare el tranguay, mayoral" in *Caras y caretas*, in 1905. The youngest of the family chose a Bohemian lifestyle whose main stage was Paris, an unavoidably short life that ended in the mountains of Córdoba, with tuberculosis, which was rampant at the time: he left one memorable tango, "Germaine," among others less recognized: "París," "Mala sombra," "Mala firma," "Perfiles criollos," "Clínicas."

A late interview paints his widow as an elderly woman come upon hard times: "I thought things would end differently [. . .] I would have liked to have been an artist," Georgette Leroy de López Buchardo sighs, recalling her times studying painting with

Anglada Camarasa in Paris. The interviewer summarizes and narrates her secrets using very few quotations in the transcript; it's impossible to know whether the story's dubious chronology should be attributed to her eroded memory or the listener's carelessness.

According to the published account, the twenty-one-year-old Alberto López Buchardo, following the Paris street festivals on the 14th of July, continues partying till the sun comes up in a *boite* where he takes over the piano and plays tangos while his friends ask the inveterate night owls to dance. "People admire the music. Tango has arrived in Paris." (In 1903?) Further along in the text there is an undated invitation by "Count and Countess of Rescke" [sic] to López Buchardo and Ricardo Güiraldes; the imminent writer shows some tango moves during the *soirée*, "simplifying them," and the people in attendance love it so much that the Princess invites them to her mansion for a "nocturnal masquerade." A friend of the musician's, referred to simply as Biaus, travels to Buenos Aires and promises: "I will send the first tango orchestra to Paris." Months later, "musicians from the *porteño* slums" arrive. I quote from the text:

> *It's morning. The musicians arrive from Marseille and it's very cold. [. . .] The butler receives them. "Monsieur is sleeping in his atelier. I can't bother him." I show up amidst the confusion and let them in. They drink hot coffee, pull out their instruments and the music breaks out right there in the morning into a tango*

that wakes up Monsieur. Alberto comes down from his atelier
thinking he's living a dream and finds the boys there. Without
interrupting them, he walks over to the piano and accompanies
them . . . A spectacular partnership is born: La China will dance
with Casimiro Aín . . .

The story offers several clues, only to immediately erase them. To start with, the name "Rescke." The correct spelling of the last name is probably Reszke and the residence in question was that of the famous baritone Jean de Reszke (1850–1925), née Jan Mieczysław in Poland, and following a distinguished international career, he retired circa 1904, to breed race horses in the country of his birth and teach voice in Paris. There he retained Henri Granpierre, architect of the Polignac family, to build a sumptuous *hôtel particulier*, and he taught several students, among whom are Adelina Patti, Bidù Sayåo, and Maggie Teyte.

Or perhaps it's his son of the same name, a painter whose work had already debuted in the Salon des Artistes Français in 1914? It's hard to imagine it being the bassist Edouard de Reszke (1853–1917), the baritone's younger son, whose less illustrious career alternated between London and Warsaw at the turn of the century, and was eclipsed before he disappeared during the First World War.

Who were those musicians coming from Marseille of a winter's morn? Other chronicles identify "La China" as being a "brunette seasoned in the 'academies' that flourished in Buenos Aires" . . .

the presence in the group of Casimiro Aín, a.k.a. "El Lecherito" or "El Vasquito" (1882–1940), allows us to identify them. Aín was a consummate dancer by the time he traveled to France in 1913; the bandoneonist Vicente Loduca traveled with him on the steamboat Sierra de la Ventana, along with the violinist Eduardo Monelos and the pianist Celestino Ferrer. According to Aín, Alberto López Buchardo had financed the trip.

The musician's widow claims that he was the one who convinced a businessman to open the Argentine Cabaret: "El Garrón." Other sources, though, refer to López Buchardo as the "intellectual creator" of the venue that would become so famous; consensus says the Cabaret Princess turned into El Garrón thanks to the initiative of the bandoneonist Manuel Pizarro, whom the Consul Vicente Madero introduced to the venue's owner. Pizarro arrived in Paris in 1921, after spending a year in Marseille; Alberto López Buchardo died in the mountains of Córdoba in 1918 . . . Did Pizarro agree with his idea? Could Madero have conveyed it to him?

López Buchardo's widow, by the way, was that same Georgette Leroy painted by Hermen (Hermenegildo) Anglada Camarasa (1872–1959). The Catalan painter, Mallorcan by adoption and originator of the "Pollensa School," lived in Paris from 1894 to 1914 with few interruptions; he painted the world of the theater and café concerts in a style between Belle-Epoque decorativism and colorful Fauve; his work was also shown in the Vienna Secession and was appreciated by Diaghilev and Meyerhold. He was closely connected to·the Argentine colony there: Alberto López Buchardo met his future wife in Camarasa's atelier, she was one of the painter's students and models; Anglada Camarasa was also a friend of Adán Diehl's (1891–1952), the Argentine poet and connoisseur who during his marriage to Delia del Carril, Pablo Neruda's future wife, was also Güiraldes's brother-in-law. (Diehl had bought a vast property in Mallorca, which became the heart of the famous Hotel Formentor, inaugurated in 1929, and which he had to sell in 1936.) And it's precisely in Mallorca where we can contemplate the face with which Georgette Leroy seduced López Buchardo, not far from that of Adelina del Carril de Güiraldes. Both portraits, painted by Anglada Camarasa, are on display in Palma de Mallorca's Fundación Caixa, where the artist's work is kept.

Whatever the case, there is little doubt that it was at Reszke's salon (to whom only Argentine sources bestow an aristocratic title) where Güiraldes dazzled high-society and aristocratic guests with his tango prowess. The Prince and Princess of Murat must have been in attendance, and the Archduke Boris of Russia, a few of the Rothschilds, Reynaldo Hahn and André Messager, among others. Güiraldes danced with one of the guests, whom eyewitnesses identified as Yvette Guetté; ignorant of the steps, she allowed herself to be guided by the poet. There are diverging accounts of the episode, even contradictory ones. The writer later elaborated on it in *Raucho – Moments of a Contemporary Youth* (1917): "A body acquiescently attached itself to his. Uneasy at first, he took simple steps, then in light of his partner's skill his courage grew and he danced unreservedly, losing himself in the rhythm. She followed him, bending to his will, foreseeing the cuts, the satin subtly slipping. Raucho steered the abandoned waist and a soft vertigo lifted in him, intensely, with the comprehension of both bodies . . ."

Dubious Testimonies

AN EVENING AT THE PALAIS DE GLACE

I'm that nocturnal gallant who danced
with you so freely in the Palé de Glas . . .
Enrique Cadícamo, Carnavales de mi vida

If the legendary Blonde Mireya was a mythical creature and not a historical one, a combination of features taken from a variety of women at the dawn of tango, and if, as has been contended, she really used to dance in Hansen's, it can hardly come as a surprise that a foundational event in milonga history in Buenos Aires has never been "factually" confirmed.

According to several writers and historians with minor variations in their tellings, the evening that heralded if not tango's induction into high society, at least its endorsement, was held by Baron Antonio de Marchi in the Palais de Glace, in 1912 or 1913.

There's not a trace of the event in any of the newspapers of the period, or in the memoirs of anyone alive at the time; only in the work of later authors who recollect hearsay, enriching the scuttlebutt with names of musicians ("Tano" Genaro's ensemble) and dancers (Saborido, Contreras).

De Marchi, athlete and milonga dancer, was married to General Roca's daughter María. According to the architect Juan Manuel Peña, longtime director of the Museo de la Ciudad and living repository of *porteño* stories, what Marchi organized in 1913, at the Palace Theater on Corrientes 957 from September 22nd to the 24th, was the first tango competition sponsored by the Sociedad Sportiva Argentina, of which the Baron was president. Six actor couples were hired to dance, sixty-three arrangements were presented in the competition, and six were chosen as finalists. This was surely the event that marked tango's initiation into "polite" society. The presence of Esther Lavallol de Roca, the General's widow and mother-in-law of the organizer, acted as guarantor for the soirée, along with the attendance of other ladies with traditional last names: Victorica, Santamarina, Quintana, Rodríguez Larreta, Lezica Alvear, Unzué, Anchorena. Julián Aguirre presided over the jury, made up of milonga-dancing *niños bien* (fun-loving sons of wealthy families) like Daniel Videla Dorna and Vicente Madero.

Peña digs out two journalistic testimonies to sustain his hypothesis. One of them was signed by "Viejo Tanguero" and published in *Crítica* on September 22, 1913, the day the competition began.

"So tonight old tango with its shameful stigma entered national life, reemerging on the aristocratic stage like Gounod's old Faust, the triumphal entrance of a *niño bien*, decked out in snob attire, immaculate tail coats and gently gloved hands." And the next day, in *La Nación*, one reads: "The inaugural evening of the tango competition in the Palace Theater, sponsored by Sociedad Sportiva Argentina, showed a lively social gathering. Sportiva's festivities appear to indicate the consecration of tango by the most illustrious figures of our society."

They both point out how, that legendary evening, a new incarnation of tango dancing was born. This smooth (or smoothed out) form was more decorous, without indelicate or explicit figures, and would be acceptable for the ballrooms, while the tango of "cuts" and "breaks" would remain the patrimony of popular culture, with an aftertaste of its seedy origins.

That Palace Theater where the legendary competition was staged is now but a shadow in the city's memory. The Palais de Glace, on the other hand, originally purposed as a cycling track and skating rink – hence its name – before the surviving structure was rebuilt in 1910, remains firmly anchored in milonga mythology. In his song "Tango de ayer," Enrique Cadícamo evokes the Royal Pigalle cabaret, which became the Tabarís on Corrientes, and also pays tribute to the Palais de Glace twice. There is "Carnavales de mi vida" and "Palais de Glace," which from the very title gives voice to an *ubi sunt*: "Palé de Glas / as of nineteen twenty / you no longer remain / with your cordial air . . . / There I danced / the tangos of my student years, / there I dreamt of the boys that came afore."

It'll be difficult to destroy the legend of that mythical evening at the Palais de Glace when the doors of tango were opened to high society, no matter how many documents there are that call it into question. I predict that it will concur with Cocteau's intuition, as so many things do: "I've always preferred myth to history, because history is made of truths that over time turn into lies, while myth is a fiction that, in the end, turns out to be true."

THE VATICAN EPISODE

Only the circumstances, the time,
and one or two names were made-up.
                    Jorge Luis Borges, "Emma Zunz"

Another legendary episode, perhaps the most extravagant in the history of milonga, has also had its legitimacy called into question. A French journalist named Emmanuel Carrère, Rome correspondent for the Parisian *Le Temps*, imagined in January of 1914 that Pope Pius X, after expressing his disapproval of the fashionable dances of the day, gave audience to a couple of married men. Later versions refer to the men as brothers or cousins – possibly belonging to the Vatican's *aristocrazia nera* (families closest to the Popes, accomplices in money-dealing and influence trafficking both in and outside the Vatican). Apparently these young men, so the story goes, danced a tango before His Holiness to prove that there was nothing indecent to the steps and figures of the aristocracy's preferred rhythm. Half-convinced, the elderly Pope, of Venetian origin, proposed they bring back the *furlana*, Veneto's olden dance, whose elegance and decorum he ordered a servant present that evening, a fellow countryman, to demonstrate.

On the 23rd and 28th of January, *Il Corriere della Sera* remarked on the news coming out of Paris, and questioned its authenticity, though without entirely challenging it. The news let loose a journalistic storm, where the *furlana* came to be known as the "Pope's dance," providing the anticlerical media with material to poke delicious fun at the Vatican, which obliged *L'Osservatore Romano* to clarify that Pius X didn't spend his time on such frivolities. In fact, while in Germany, the Kaiser himself proclaimed the censure of tango, in Italy the subject remained within the confines of bishops and pastors. (In 1967, the historian Guillermo Gallardo, in his guise as the president of the Junta de Historia Eclesiástica, a branch of the Argentine Episcopate, answered a query made by José Gobello, President of the Buenos Aires Academy of Lunfardo, confirming that a document exists in the Holy See that would have prohibited tango dancing.)

The legend would live on as doggedly as the mythical evening at the Palais de Glace, or the dubious existence of the Blonde Mireya.

Once out of the bag, the story of Pius X's tango-dancing episode spread so widely that it became the subject of a stage production. Some clubs tried to bring the furlana and its convoluted movements back into vogue with lackluster results; young Italians from "respectable families" parodied the dance. And in the meantime the tango had settled in amongst them without much risk of being deposed; the British writer Sir Harold Acton remembers the leisurely young boys of Roman society given over to the tango, "their unemotional virility in sharp contrast to a shining wrist watch, a shimmer of rings and a silk handkerchief steeped in Coty perfume." In Paris, Angel Villoldo composed a tango to mark the occasion: "Salve furlana." On the 7th of February, *L'Illustration* published an engraving showing the Pope on his throne watching a couple dancing tango; "*se non è vero . . .*" the quote suggests, keeping its distance with the traditional Italian phrase as a pretense to fabrication. A French version of the episode suggests that Cardinal Merry de Val, one of Pius X's trusted French prelates, counseled His Holiness on behalf of a Roman Prince who happens to be a tango enthusiast, to give the dance his blessing. To convince him, the prelate arranges for a young couple to perform a bowdlerized choreography to convince him, the woman clad in an ankle-length skirt, her shoulders and head veiled in a lace mantilla.

Eventually, the story of tango being danced before the Pope found its way into Julien Green's memoir of his childhood and adolescence, which he wrote in English during the Second World War when he found a haven in the country of his birth. He describes the furlana in *Memories of Happy Days*, which a man and woman dance two or three feet apart from each other, preferably holding a handkerchief, and the book closes with what could only be read as a sort of epitaph: "Parisians looked on and grinned, their faith in tango unperturbed."

Pius X died a few months after this imaginary audience. There's an Argentine postscript to the story: a decade later, when Doctor García Mansilla was the Argentine ambassador to the Holy See, on February 1 1924, at nine in the morning, Casimo Aín, "El Vasquito," danced one of the Canaro brothers' tangos, called *Ave María*, for Pius XI . . . His partner was a former librarian and translator for the Argentine embassy at the time; he wore a tailcoat, she a long skirt and nun's shoes. The couple was careful not to give their backs to His Holiness as they moved, and their demonstration came to an end with both kneeling before Her. Aín's memory of the event is the only promise of truth we have regarding the episode, which was recorded by Manuel Castelló. Doctor García Mansilla, on the other hand, didn't record the account in his memoirs.

1914 and Afterwards

Das Leben starb. Dir Mörder tanzen Tango.
(Life died. The assassins dance tango.)

Karl Kraus, *Tod und Tango*

The year preceding the First World War would come to be seen as the end of the world more than as the end of an epoch. The European summer of 1914 arrives, and the Argentine colony abandons Paris. Most of them beat a hasty return to Buenos Aires and scatter, some travel via Mallorca with no established dates of arrival.

When war is declared, austerity measures imposed on public leisure put a damper on social activities and summon rules of decorum free of excess or eccentricities. Any display of foreign fashion raises distrustful eyebrows and becomes semi-clandestine. Of course none of this prevents the narrator of *In Search of Lost Time*, looking for shelter during an air raid, from finding an establishment where a sadomasochist drama stages its mercantile comedy. But the "madness" of 1913 had suddenly acquired an attractive marginality.

Tango continued to be danced in more or less underground establishments. According to one journalist at the time, "one had to resort to the most unforeseen locations to dance it." Not to mention certain houses whose shutters were kept closed to drown out the sound of violins and pianos. Anyplace was fair game: taverns, hangars, artist studios; the persecuted dancers would gather in the outskirts of town and even the slums with "the faith of martyrs."

In the postwar years and immediately afterwards, the years they call "roaring," the tango would become a trend among a much wider public, stripping it of its charms as a novelty and clandestine activity. In surrealist Robert Desnos's first book, *Prospectus*, published in 1919 at nineteen years of age, the principal themes are exoticism and worldliness. Playing with ideas of fashion and worldliness, the word "tango" (which in French carries the stress on the last vowel) is repeated in each stanza, rhyming with the name Margot and with the principality of Monaco. Valentino danced a tango in *The Four Horsemen of the Apocalypse* and the scene, which incited hilarity in Argentina, was seen by the rest of the world as a stylized erotic ritual. The star's movements were imbued with a dreamlike sensuality: gaucho or sheik, bullfighter or Hindu prince, Valentino couldn't or shouldn't take part in anything that had the aspect of his audience's daily life.

That brand of manly sensuality couldn't help but aggravate men who felt irrevocably out of range. In 1920, before referring to "stinking Argentine tangos" in his novel *El cura de Monleón* (*The Priest of Monleón*, 1936), Pío Baroja had already written in *La sensualidad pervertida*, subtitled: *Ensayos amorosos de un hombre ingenuo en una época de decadencia* (*Perverted Sensuality: Amorous Essays of a Naïve Man in an Age of Decadence*): "There were a few professional Argentine tango dancers present, tall Americans, brown, shaven, dressed in black with wide-brimmed hats: all flashy types or half-flashy, dancing as if they were in a priesthood." Keep in mind that Baroja was short, red-haired, bearded, and addicted to wearing his beret.

Free from the tyranny of novelty, tango was then earmarked for its true cult following. From 1921 till his early death in 1924, Arolas performed in Paris accompanied by French musicians; as happens with poets and explorers, the "tiger of the bandoneon" would become a legend and enjoy prestige only after his death. The utmost act of public esteem came on April 23, 1925, when Francisco Canaro, already a celebrity in Buenos Aires, debuted in the cabaret Florida on rue de Clichy, where Gardel would debut in France three years later. During his stay, Canaro played at a reception for President Poincaré, saw the violinist Jascha Heifetz dance tango (who he thought did quite well), and was commissioned to entertain on fashion designer Paul Poiret's three *péniches*, which he had decorated and anchored on the bank of the Seine as part of the Exposition des Arts Décoratifs, cradle of Art Deco. Caldarella and the Scarpino brothers composed "Canaro en París" to celebrate these eventful days.

For some, Poiret, who designed the set and wardrobe for Richepin's comedy, had invented the "tango color," a very bright orange with a touch of pink or saffron. To others, what Poiret invented was an article of clothing – part skirt, part pants – called "tango" thanks to slits up the side of each leg, which allowed for freedom of movement; and also the "tango blouse," made from a single cut of silk or satin with a seam running from the shoulder to the wrist.

There's another, more interesting legend regarding the color tango: an oriental fabrics importer decided to use the name of the fashion trend to help sell off his stock of yellowish-orange silk that had been ruined in a warehouse. Those were the years when blending beer and grenadine was called a "tango cocktail" and a train from Paris to Deauville was called the "Tango Express." In 1918, the Stade Levallois-Mayenne soccer team chose the color tango for its team shirt; and tales of another act of cunning regarding the incident are still told today: at first, apparently the club had chosen a blood-red color for their jerseys, but it quickly faded and so to avoid being teased over having pink uniforms, they decided to call the team's color "tango" . . . Another colorful story is told in *Esvén*, Arturo Jacinto Alvarez's barely fictionalized memoir: the color was inspired by a group of kids who dressed up as little devils for Count Etienne de Beaumont's party; their red costumes were drenched in a sudden downpour, but were quickly dried and pressed with hot irons, which faded the color to the point of discovering, or inventing, the color tango.

It was precisely during last century's aughts when "cultivated" musicians began composing tangos. It's not the case with Albéniz: "Tango," the second piece in his piano suite *España* (1905), op. 165, is clearly an Andalusian tango. In Satie's tango, from the piano suite *Sports et divertissements* (1914, published in 1923), the Andalusian reminiscences are closer to the habanero than the Argentine tango danced in Paris. In Stravinsky's *L'Histoire du soldat* (1918), on the other hand, a syncopated tango is one of the suite's three dances, identifiable for an ear accustomed to dancing it (the other two are a waltz and ragtime). Weill went on to compose two tangos the following decade: "Tango-ballade," sung in his *Dreigroschenoper* (1928), later reworked into an instrumental composition for the orchestra suite *Kleine Dreigroschenmusik*, and also "Tango der Matrosen" ("The Sailor's Tango") for *Happy End* (1929); later, during his French exile, he would compose "Youkali Tango," a theme forgotten for a long time before finally being recovered, which began as incidental music for Jacques Deval's *Marie Galante* (1934).

It's impossible to touch on the popularity of Argentine tango orchestras in France in the 1920's without mentioning a character rich in fictional material: the violinist Eduardo Bianco.

After playing with the Manuel Pizarro ensemble in 1923, Bianco joined Juan "Bachicha" Deambroggio to form the popular Bianco-Bachicha orchestra. By 1926 he had his own orchestra, though they continued to be connected through the publishing imprint they'd set up, Les Editions Musicales Bianco-Bachicha.

Born in Rosario in 1892, Eduardo Bianco showed an early vocation for the upper spheres: his first tangos were dedicated to Alejandro Menéndez Behety and to "Macoco" Alzaga Unzué; later, in 1927, he would dedicate his most famous tango, "Plegaria," to Alfonso XIII. After playing for crowned heads in the twenties, he didn't spurn admiration by Mussolini and Goebbels, performed for Hitler in Berlin in 1939, and toured the countries occupied by the Third Reich.

"Plegaria," renamed in Germany as "Todestango" (the tango of death), had the dubious privilege of being music the SS troupes forced the Jewish prisoner bands to play in the Janowska camp, near Lvov, generally with flute, clarinet, and accordion, the typical ensemble for klezmer music. . . . In Auschwitz, the prisoner bands were forced to play what they called "the tango of death," either the original composition or another one they gave the same name, as a prelude to the mass executions.

Under investigation by the British intelligence services in 1944, Bianco obtained a Spanish visa to leave Europe and return to Buenos Aires where his music couldn't compete with Pichuco, Fresedo, Pugliese, Di Sarli, and De Caro; Cadícamo aired publicly that Bianco had worked for the Wehrmacht through 1942. In 1950, now back in Europe – Atilio Stampone remembers, who joined the orchestra when he was twenty-one – Bianco saw for himself that people were no longer interested in tango: now the rage was for boogie-woogie, swing, anything that had the North American sound. The orchestra came to the end of its musical career doing tours throughout the Middle East: in Lebanon and Egypt they found an audience faithful to the Argentine tango and even had the chance to play for King Faruk. Bianco died in 1959.

"That Brothel Reptile"

The real Tango in all the antique effrontery of its ingeniousness, proves that the heroic age, made up of the naïf and the barbarous, is fast losing its last vestiges of character in the wilderness of civilized monotony. Le Tango is disappearing.

Georges Clemenceau, 1911

A century ago, the future Prime Minister of France lamented tango's gradual disappearance, victim of what he saw as a dreary, civilized monotony...

Tango's fall into decadence: a subject frequented by succeeding generations. The novelty of one generation becomes classic, if not conventional, for the next; new twists come along, but they're generally received unenthusiastically, more symptoms of decadence.

Admittedly, the traditional form of tango suffered an eclipse between the 60s and mid-80s, specifically as a popular dance – a period of time that not insignificantly happens to coincide with Piazzolla's most fertile experiments – yet all the grief over its so-called decadence has suspiciously, and all too often, seemed like some baleful elegy to lost youth, a requiem intoned by those who would rather not admit that the world is in constant transformation as they are aging.

What I find significant in Clemenceau's observation, made while visiting a proud, opulent Argentina preparing the stage for its Centennial festivities, is that he points to "*l'antique impudeur de sa naïveté*" as a quality being lost in tango. Might he have hazarded while in Buenos Aires, a jaunt to some last corral where they still dance that archaic form of milonga that had already begun morphing into tango?

⸻

Borges, subservient to the cult of bravery, to the glorification of man with knife in hand, pined for this festive, rabble-rousing dance form, the sparring *guapos* capable of dancing it on any street corner. "Along the street, good folks squander / their vulgar words, the sweetest talk / to the beat of a tango called "La morocha" / two plebs show off their agile cuts" (Carriego). To dance on a tile: to some it's the heroic feat in a tenement yard; to others it's a prison exercise in the tiny space of a cell.

It's hard to draw a line between the young Borges's longing for strong experience, tagged by his parents as a writer yet confined to the sanctuary of the family library by his own insecurity, and the ideological elaboration of that desire: contempt for sentimentalism, or what he perceived as pretense (which Coronel Borges's grandson read as being the influence of immigrants and rowdy arrivistes) and that Italian temperament in art, to which he was impervious.

It seems to me that only a passing sightseer could find at once *impudor* (immodesty) and *inocencia* (naïvete) in primitive forms of tango. As happens so frequently on stage, frontal lighting squashes and flattens, while lateral lighting that creates depth, allows one to perceive volume. At the first half of the 19th century and from their tangential viewpoints, the Marquis de Custine in Russia and Tocqueville in the U.S., were able to see what familiarity had rendered indiscernible to others. In tango, Ricardo Güiraldes, Vicente Madero, and Daniel Videla Dorna looked splendid on the dance floors of Paris, *niños bien* so sure of their place in society that they could indulge any transgression ("never explain, never apologize"), while other Argentines, some with the same social origins but who felt more closely identified with the culture of the Centennial ("*Rien ne tue un homme comme d'être obligé de représenter un pays . . .*" Jacques Vaché / Nothing kills a person like being forced to represent a country), preferred to reject tango; or rather, the European tango craze and how it became identified with Argentina.

Tango had come up from the streets, from the more-or-less back room brothels, from cabarets of dubious status. In a culture where men from "high society" could go slumming with "lowlifes," women's roles were cleanly divided into those obliged to ignore the behavior and those who practiced it. All curiosity on the part of the former for how the latter danced could only point to curiosity, to barely veiled desire, to animate sensuality.

The Centennial festivities coincided with the consolidation of human trafficking in Buenos Aires through its two principal networks: the French in Marseille and the Jews in Zwi Migdal. The spread of tango throughout Europe, a craze that took hold despite dogged censure, was an outrage to those who lived as agents for an Argentina that was not only wealthy, but irreproachable, where culture was part of its decorum. In 1933, in *Radiografía de la pampa*, Martínez Estrada spares nothing when talking about its origins: "When it was practiced in the slums of the outskirts . . . its cachet was limited to houses of ill-repute. It was only music; a lascivious kind of music that bore implicit the lyrics that would materialize years later, when the popular crowd that liked it could finally produce its poets."

The dance's cathouse origins still troubled the imagination of all Argentines for being still so recent. The comforting illusion of a pristine interior (criollo, traditionalist) faced with a corrupt capital (cosmopolitan, innovative) fed the anger of a wide variety of writers, in whom the flames of an as yet unarticulated political system, a reactionary utopia, were being fanned: that single-minded "return to the land" that Petain would preach in 1940 armed with words, and Pol-Pot in 1975, with firearms.

The delusion began incubating as a reaction against the waves of immigrants that arrived in the decade of the 1880's. Traditional criollo families saw the massive influx of foreigners (poor foreigners, unfamiliar with the etiquette of the "great village," colorful in appearance, boisterous) as a corrupting influence: believing they had a nefarious effect on customs and also on the stock market, bringing a crisis in 1890. This is the subject of novels that are only read today as documents of social history: *¿Inocentes o culpables?* (*Innocent or Guilty?*, 1884) by Antonio Argerich and *En la sangre* (*In the Blood*, 1887) by Eugenio Cambaceres use caricatures of Italian immigrants, an "inferior race," as the target of their insults; *La bolsa* (*The Stock Exchange*, 1891) by Julián Martel predicts another apocalypse: "The race of Semites, always slithering like a snake, will nonetheless prevail over the Arian race."

Miguel Cané, author of *Juvenilia*, more restrained and pragmatic, links the "foreign hoi-polloi" to the period's revolutionary ideas, the first trade unions formed by immigrant workers; as a senator in 1899, he proposed a bill that would allow for the expulsion of "undesirable" foreigners; passed in 1902, it became known as the Law of Residency. "Honor and respect the pure vestiges of our national assembly; every day we are fewer Argentines. Safeguard our legitimate predominance. . . . Let's close the circle and watch over it."

In this context, tango arrives as the urban form of music *par excellence*, the dance of a city turning cosmopolitan, anarchistic, and unmanageable. The new Buenos Aires becomes the focus of scorn by those who feel they're losing their grip on it, pining for an agrarian society that would conserve the spiritual values and lifestyle uncontaminated by the flood of immigrants. 1910 arrives with its triumphalist staging of the Centennial and a book is published, halfway between a novel and an essay, meant to draw a controversy: *El Diario de Gabriel Quiroga* (*The Diary of Gabriel Quiroga*) by Manuel Gálvez. (Earlier versions were subtitled: "*Homenaje a la Patria en el Centenario de su Revolución independentista*" / "Homage to the Homeland on the Centenary of the Revolution of Independence.") "I know I'll strike a dissonant note among all the eulogies, all the cosmopolitan flattery and homegrown vanity that will assault my homeland," the author declares not without a tone of self-satisfaction. "But I'm not afflicted . . . this volume is in a way a political book."

It's no coincidence that in this book, Gálvez airs his disgust with immigrant music. He ordains an illustrious lineage that places tango in opposition to what has yet to be termed *folklore*. "The coastland has forgotten its music. The immigrants, by displacing the gauchos, have done away with the criollo songs and dances . . . In its place we now have tango, the product of cosmopolitanism, music that is hybrid and vile. I know of nothing as repugnant as Argentine tango. The dance is grotesque . . . and represents the highest proponent of national vulgarity . . . one hears that ugly, anti-artistic music everywhere, like a penance, a deplorable symptom of our nation being torn apart."

Gálvez also inscribed himself into another no less distinguished lineage: the tango's *odi et amo*. In his dotage as a writer, he would publish memoirs where he admitted his youthful attraction to that music with its "taste of sin." "Around 1904 or 1905, I played tangos on the piano at Leopoldo Lugones's *tertulia*. Slum dancing came easy to me. Nothing peculiar about it: I felt its music and from 1900 to 1901 I played tango on the piano. When people heard me playing they were astonished to see me, a 'distinguished young man' playing slum music with such flair. So I danced it, and rather well, 'with a great amount of sentiment,' according to my female abettors. You see I really did feel it; I felt its soul, its color, its taste of sinfulness, its hypocritical voluptuousness."

———

Enrique (Rodríguez) Larreta, author of *La Gloria de Don Ramiro*, a highly successful Hispanicizing pastiche when it was published, served as Argentina's ambassador to France between December 1910 and October 1916. The tango rage in Paris hit its zenith during the years immediately prior to the First World War. Interviewed on the subject, Larreta came up with a way to equipoise contempt for the dance and respect for the "city of lights" where that dance "from the pigsties" was being introduced into salon society. "That's right, tango is danced in our country," he declared, "but not in the *pampas*, in certain bigger cities, and more than anywhere else, Buenos Aires: it's a dance reserved particularly for the brothels: from which it has emerged solely to take Europe by storm. . . . In a city like Paris, the most delicate and refined, they could never dance tango like pigsty swine from Buenos Aires. It's the same dance, the same gestures, the same contortions; but to be sure the Parisians add moderation, and criteria as only they know how, which is what makes nothing impossible for them . . ." Let's not forget that those were the Parisian years when the poet Rubén Darío oversaw the magazine *Elegancias*, being both a style guide and a mirror of high society for the rich South Americans who spent part of the year in the "city of lights."

And so nobody would suspect him of tolerance, Larreta defends the honor of his diplomatic mission: "There's at least one ballroom in Paris where Argentine tango is not danced, and that's the one at the Argentine delegation." He was even pithier on another occasion: "In Buenos Aires, tango is a dance exclusive to the cathouses and worst variety of lowlife bars. It's never danced in the ballrooms of polite society or among distinguished people. To Argentine ears, tango music rouses truly distasteful ideas."

—

The restraint exercised by the career diplomat writer pales in comparison with the outrage of another writer, who took it upon himself to act as cultural ambassador. While Larreta declared *las pampas* virgin territory free of tango, relegating that licentious music to specific urban centers, particularly the debauched capital, Leopoldo Lugones began by declaring that "gaucho music" is the opposite of tango, and that tango doesn't "belong to our family," which he wrote in French for *La Revue sud-américaine*, whose seven issues (January to July of 1914) he oversaw in Paris: "*Quoi fu'il en soit, si par la musique on peut juger de l'esprit d'un people; si la musique est, comme je le crois, la revelation la plus sincere de son caractère, le lecteur apprendra à connaître le gaucho par les morceaux typiques qui suivent. Leur brio elegant, leur grace légère, leur delicatessen sentimentale lui révèleront, entre autres choses, que le tango n'est pas de la famille . . .*"

Lugones, who would become the Argentine representative at the Assembly for Intellectual Cooperation of the Society of Nations, conducted an analysis of the so-called "character" of the Argentine people through its musical forms. In 1913, he gave a series of conferences at the Odeon theater where he acknowledged that Martin Fierro and the figure of the gaucho are personifications of the Argentine soul. In 1916 he gathered these ideas into *El payador*: "If the spirit of a people is revealed in its music; if it is, as I believe it to be, the most genuine revelation of the national character, then it's the gaucho that is revealed through it. The elegant brio of their compositions, their nimble gracefulness and subtle sentimentality, they're what define *criollo* music today and anticipate the *criollo* music of tomorrow. In its intrinsically light style one finds the secret of a higher purpose, not so in the contortions of tango, that brothel reptile, so unfairly labeled as Argentine during the shameless period it was in vogue. The potent dominance of rhythm in our dances is, I repeat, a condition of virility that carries with it the brute ability to breed. Keeping a respected space from the partner's body is possible and gallant, thanks to the rhythm that governs the pantomime that way, instead of acting like her pimp, which is what happens in tango, meant only to beat out a provocative wiggle, or the misguided caginess of an embrace, bodies held so close together as obliged by the dance, and what defines its true character."

Lugones's phrase "that brothel reptile" became so famous that the second part was left in the shade, less colorful perhaps, but more resonant in the long run: "so unfairly labeled as Argentine." And in that second part he announces, once and for all, the Maurras-style nationalism that had been incubating. A year later, one of its most eloquent spokespersons, Carlos Ibarguren (Uriburu), would take on the issue of the city-countryside dichotomy, specifically repudiating the idea supported by Europeans that only a "hybrid and mixed-race" dance could capture the Argentine character. (A character concurrent with the city where tango was born: in 1895, 52% of the population in Buenos Aires hadn't been born in Argentina; in 1890, 18% of the population lived in tenements, and though by 1914, 60% of families were home owners, over 50% of them were not Argentine nationals.)

Ibarguren writes: "An illegitimate product, lacking any scent of wilderness or the land's natural grace, but instead a rich slice of some tenement slum in the outskirts, has spread throughout the world to the delight of a many-hued clientele in European hotels and live music cafés in the great capital cites; tango, whose patent the world gave to Argentina, drawing an association that isn't really there. Tango is not properly Argentine; it's a hybrid, or multi-racial product that was born in the slums, it draws on a blend of the tropical habanera and a doctored form of milonga. How far the crude squirm of tango is from the noble, distinguished cueca (Chilean national dance), performed with aristocratic mimicry similar to that of the pavana or the minuet!"

＊

This unexpected appreciation of the cueca's aristocratic character and its connection with the pavana's and the minuet's wasn't the only time the sternest right and the stiffest left would find common ground. If Lugones anticipated Mussolini in admiring "a condition of virility that carries with it the brute ability to breed," a kind of virility the poet seemed to notice in folkloric dances as opposed to the "misguided caginess of an embrace," characteristic of the tango, Leónidas Barletta, member of the Communist Party in Argentina during Stalin's rule, venerable founder and director of El Teatro del Pueblo throughout tragic times, throws light on the subject through the prism of class consciousness without keeping himself from expressing notions of hygiene and, again, virility.

"Tango is a jeremiad of effeminates, the late-blooming woman unaware of her femininity. It's the music of degenerates who refuse to wear their proletarian clothes, whose greasy-haired women leave factories for the brothels. Tango is unhealthy. The sensuality that prevails is one of inhibition, coyness, and fear. The music of other nations is categorically sensual, ingeniously sensual. In tango sensuality is bogus, artificially crafted." (Compare this with Marinetti: "in the name of health, of strength, of willpower, of virility, we abhor tango and its tiresome walkabouts.")

As so often throughout the history of the left, and not only in Argentina, the notion of "a people" here is used as a mere ideological construct: Barletta courageously and tenaciously believed in and defended a form of theater that is already evident in its very name; at the same time, he preferred to ignore the expression of a people disinclined toward his historical teleology. (I haven't been able to locate the original text or where it was published, it's been repeated by a wide variety of scholars, always taking as their source Horacio Salas's *El tango*.)

⁓

A sense of vicarious satisfaction, a sort of payback by proxy, comes with the discovery that in the twenties of last century, a protectionist ruling by the French musicians' union banned foreign musicians from playing there, save in sporadic performances while on tour. The injunction obliged the Argentine orchestras already present in Paris, like Manuel Pizarro's and Genaro Espósito's, along with the most popular of them all at the time, Bianco-Bachicha's, to dress up in gaucho outfits so as to be considered a variety show and thereby dodge the zealous union's protectionism.

That's how an impure, "denationalized" (Gálvez) form of music, a civilian music of immigrants and brothels, came to be played in Paris by troops of costumed gauchos whose get-ups, rich in materials and ornamental paraphernalia, stylistically depicted the kind of purebred creoles that Lugones, Larreta, Gálvez, and Ibarguren had rallied around, in opposition to the obscene deluge of the milonga.

⁓

Impervious to its prosecutors, that "brothel reptile" would develop a thick, resilient skin for its still supple body. Capable of surviving the convulsions of taste and society, capable of changing color and seducing those who hadn't heard the condemnation of judges half a century ago, it fed off of its adversaries, defiantly flaunting the self-same features with which they had tried to discredit it.

Tango slithered its way into the academic world towards the end of the 20th century, in studies called "gender" or more widely, "cultural." Julie Taylor, professor of anthropology at Rice University and a professional dancer, published *Paper Tangos* in 1998, in which she proposes a political study and analysis of social violence through the perspective of her own personal experience on stage and on the dance floor. Marta Elena Savigliano, a professor of anthropology and "political theorist" in the World Arts and Culture Department of UCLA, published in 1995 *Tango and the Political Economy of Passion*, and in 2003, *Angora Matta*, a bilingual fiction in the form of a thriller that investigates through a feminist and ethnographic perspective, the current passion for tango. She also wrote an analysis of Sally Potter's film, *The Tango Lesson* (1997): "Buenos Aires currently enjoys a boom in international tourism and tango is undoubtedly a main local attraction. . . . Tango promises strong, violent emotional turmoil, erotically tamed via 'universal' laws of heterosexuality and homosociality. An irresistible cinematic formula for sex tourism."

Following decades of singles dancing, which coincides with the illusory "sexual liberation" of the 60s and devolves Eros to mere physiology, the milonga now allows club scene creatures the chance to become reacquainted with the embrace and the staging of intersexual rapport: beyond the sacrosanct formula of a man imposing steps and a woman submitting to them, tango expresses a nearly mocking version of masculine passivity before the variations and embellishments with which the woman responds to his steps, variations, and embellishments, which are moves he never suggested. (Giorgio Agamben, after visiting several milongas in Buenos Aires in 2006, arrived at the conclusion that it's the woman who dominates the situation, who "leads.") And taking it beyond the playful notions of submission and domination, danced tango proclaims the only real truth in any sexual relationship, indulging and often uplifting it: the dialogue between bodies. "The tangled couple, their shoulders motionless, performs the slow Argentine walk" (Cocteau: *Portraits-souvenir: 1900–1914*).

The dance is back and its sanctuaries are sprouting like mushrooms around the city, though it no longer looks like the dance that saw its birth, even if it bears its name. Like anything with a strong personality, it boasts about what had roused such hostility and repudiation; as if declaring, defiantly: what you vilified is precisely my source of pride.

Impure, hybrid, sensual, at times morbid, at others aggressive, cultivated by Italian and Jewish immigrants and their descendants, who through it have given music to a sentiment, perhaps even an · identity in Buenos Aires that no *cueca*, no *payador*, could ever have expressed.

Clandestine Tango

1. AN EXERCISE IN URBAN ARCHAEOLOGY

The nobility of a mansion
is measured by the quality of its ghosts.

E. C., *Citizen Langlois*

I come to a standstill in front of number 777 on Lavalle Street. It's a bazaar without the pretension of an outlet: track suits, yoga pants, t-shirts, and sneakers that imitate famous brands, hair clips and sunglasses designed with an eye for fantasy, a fuchsia, heart-shaped pillow says I LOVE YOU, wigwagging fiber optic shrubberies, indescribable objects of dubious practical utility and uncertain decorative intent: an unwitting museum of low-life consumerism or underpaid handiwork from southeast Asia, stockpiled without seeking to entice shoppers who aspire to anything more than the street food sausages and pimps that colonize the street outside.

At one point, Lavalle Street had been the "Broadway of Buenos Aires," the same way Rosario had once been considered the "Argentine Chicago": guileless testaments pronounced innocently, expressing an inferiority complex. Before film theaters found refuge in the bunkers of shopping malls, the ones along Lavalle had a very distinctive personality: the Monumental was the "cathedral of *criollo* cinema," the Ocean was earmarked for large box office hits, the Arizona and the Electric, the dual features of "action" and "suspense."

The side stairs and forged metal railings have survived at 777, as have the marble, and the discreet metal letters in the style of art deco along its exterior: a seemingly odd frame for the barrage of useless goods. This architecture, those materials, the letters perpendicular to the façade, announce that this had once been the Ambassador theater. A rickety wall raised in what had been the orchestra stalls hides the stage and screen.

Before the traditional form of exhibiting the spectacle of film fell into decadence, this playhouse had screened smaller pictures than the ones shown at the Ocean, hoping to appeal to a more select audience. Its screen never pooh-poohed Argentine films like *Hay que casar a Niní* or *La guerra gaucha*, though the theater's personality could best be defined by pictures like Wyler's *The Letter* in the 40s, along with others like Powell's *The Tales of Hoffmann*, Kurosawa's *Rashomon* or Bergman's *Smiles of a Summer Night* in the 50s, or Antonioni's *La notte* of the 60s.

To construct the Ambassador, inaugurated in 1933, they first had to demolish one of Victoria Ocampo's grandfathers' homes, a structure composed of several different spaces and patios. (One hundred meters down the street, another old-style house, built in a fanciful architectural style, was still squeezed between movie theaters and bars into the 70s; it had belonged to Dardo Rocha.) It was there, in that house, where Ocampo learned how to dance the tango, in the arms of an illustrious *milonguero*: Ricardo Güiraldes.

2. TENACIOUS GHOSTS

The aristocratic ballrooms of the great capital city [Paris]
unreservedly host a dance whose vile tradition precludes its
name from even being pronounced in local salons . . . Will Paris,
which sets the standard for everything, end up forcing
high society to accept our Argentine tango?

El Hogar magazine, Buenos Aires,
December 20, 1911

VICTORIA OCAMPO DANCES THE TANGO

I knew from certain hushed whispers
and the horrified raising of eyebrows that tango
was supposed to be a naughty dance.

Julien Green, *Memories of Happy Days*, 1942

"Once carnival is here, tango becomes lord and master of all dance programs, because the dance is so libertine it can only be tolerated during these days of madness," the magazine *Caras y Caretas* declares in its issue of March 11, 1905. The note, titled "The Dance in Vogue" and illustrated by five photographs of men and women dancing tango with their hats on, explains that "the plebeians and the gentry come together in a fraternal hug" to sport "so lascivious a dance," "the working-class dance *par excellence*." And it observes precisely how: "The couples glide along swaying rhythmically to the music's beat, voluptuously, as if all their desire was delivered into that dance . . ."

At seventy-four years of age, Victoria Ocampo remembered: "The tango I was first exposed to came through a filter, like so many other things. I wasn't very partial to that ever-plaintive melody and its deliberate, stalled rhythm, the way it dragged along. I only began to like tango – and how! – by dancing it. Through dancing tango, I discovered the inimitable Argentine character. In the good sense and the bad. They didn't dance tango in Buenos Aires ballrooms, neither did adolescents from the classes nowadays so vilified. I saw it danced for the first time (oh profanity!) in my grandfather's house, Lavalle 777 (today the Ambassador cinema). The mansion, with its patios and magnolia trees in the backyard, suffered the periodic invasion of thirty-two rambunctious grandchildren of all ages. . . . The oldest grandson got a girlfriend. An exceptional tango dancer himself, one day, taking scrupulous precautions not to get caught, he astonished us dancing a tango with his girlfriend. We locked ourselves into a little room in Lavalle (smack in what is now the Ambassador's seating area) where the adults rarely ventured. The couple danced face to face amid a nearly religious silence. That was my first sight of tango and I couldn't understand why they would prohibit such a solemn dance.

Years passed, and the time came when every Thursday, come

rain or come shine, the 'Pibe de la Paternal' (Fresedo) and his group of friends would come over to my house. We would dance tango all through the afternoon and into the early evening. Ricardo Güiraldes and Vicente Madero were the champs of these memorable *jornadas*. The latter was a genius and I don't think anyone could have outdone him. When he walked the tango, his whole body, as if motionless, followed the rhythm elastically, alive with it, linking his partner in to it, minding a perfect and compassed step, as if infected by it and overtaken. Little did it matter that the lyrics to those tangos were sappy and over-the-top. They were redeemed by dancers as perfect as Vicente and Ricardo."

Ocampo's testimony doesn't offer a precise date for that "first sight of tango" or the Thursday milongas. "Years passed" is all she says. How many? Was it before or after the First World War?

VICENTE MADERO AND MANUEL PIZARRO

Vicente Madero, who Victoria Ocampo called an "insuperable" dancer, was also celebrated by Enrique Cadícamo, author of the lyrics and musical composition of *Tango de ayer*. "This was *le tango* with *porteño* roots / when Corrientes y Maipú was Montmartre, / the border crosser made a stunning goal in Paris / and off to Cabaret Garrón we went to dance. / That tango in a tux cast a spell on the woman, / it was the dapper dancer Vicente Madero."

Madero, son of Francisco Madero, Vice-President of Roca between 1880 and 1886, was the Argentine Consul in Paris when he exclaimed – Manuel Pizarro recalls – "long live Argentine tango!" as the music broke out, bashful, almost hesitant, before the debut audience. Was it perhaps in 1921? Or 1922? In the Princesse? Energized, Pizarro and his orchestra threw themselves into a rendition of *La morocha*, and seeing the audience's passionate response, apparently repeated it eight times.

Pizarro met Madero when he arrived in Paris from Marseille. He had run into Canaro on Corrientes Street one night in 1920. Lombart, the French agent, had asked "Pirincho" to recommend an orchestra, an authentic Argentine ensemble to play in France. Pizarro reached out to "El Tano" Genaro Espósito and that was how the Genaro-Pizarro orchestra was born. The French violinist Víctor Jachia accompanied them on the cargo ship, but died on the way. They arrived in Marseille on the 6th of August 1920, and performed in the Tabaris cabaret. They signed a one-year contract, poorly remunerated. In 1921, Pizarro decided to try his luck in Paris.

The Genaro-Pizarro Orchestra played at the Dauphine Pavilion and the Fontaine until Pizarro met the "incomparable" tango-dancing Consul. Madero introduced him to a man named Volterra, owner of the Princesse, and so launched the bandoneonista, orchestra director and composer's French career. Displeased with the trio he'd formed with Celestino Ferrer on piano and Güerino

Filipotto on bandoneon ("they played by ear and in the style of 1914"), Pizarro proposed a ten-piece orchestra to Volterra, drawing on musicians who played in the Princesse's jazz ensemble and who he'd train for tango, together with "El Tano" Espósito; others were Argentines passing through the city like Juan José Castro, a student at the time. Soon thereafter, the Princesse became El Garrón, the "Argentine Cabaret," which opened at ten in the evening and closed at six in the morning – with a helping of chicken stew.

The new name was probably Madero's idea; regardless, it consecrated the dance's brothel origins: "garrón" – which today defines a man who tries to obtain something without paying for it, from the verb "garronear" (to freeload, sponge) – originally described the free romp a prostitute would give to her pimp. Pizarro played at El Garrón by night, and Sans Souci in the afternoons, which was owned by the adventurer Alexandre Staviski, whose name lives on thanks to Enrique Santos Discépolo and Alain Resnais.

Madero and Güiraldes weren't the only *niños bien* who became distinguished *milongueros*. Daniel Videla Dorna and Francisco Ducasse also excelled at tango dancing, before history, or merely age, nudged them on to other horizons. (Videla Dorna, for example, became close to Julio Irazusta and Ernesto Palacio at the *Nueva República* newspaper and the Republican League, where the anti-imperialist nationalism of the 20s was sketched out; the group briefly supported Uriburu's coup before distancing itself from his government. As a deputy of the National Democratic Party during Manuel Fresco's administration in the Province of Buenos Aires, he oversaw the General Directorate of Physical Education.)

Madero was less concerned with politics, though, and he introduced Pizarro to the Ambassador Marcelo Torcuato de Alvear. Same as how he had launched Pizarro's French career by introducing him to the owner of the Princesse, he now inadvertently prompted Pizarro's return to Argentina. Alvear, as President elect in 1922, asked Pizarro to accompany him on his return to Buenos Aires to lighten up the evenings aboard the Massilia. The Genaro-Pizarro orchestra disbanded and shortly afterwards, "El Tano" put together the Orchestre Argentine Genaro Espósito, which continued to perform successfully until 1939.

(Pizarro, despite such distinguished company, could never be found far from Paris: a few years later he would return to the scene of his greatest successes; he went on to manage several cabarets, even the Montecarlo where Gardel would perform. The Second World War caught him by surprise in Alexandria; he was forced to return to Buenos Aires in an Egyptian cargo ship, though he was back in Paris by 1951. Born in the neighborhood of Almagro in 1895, he died in Nice in 1982. "El Tano" Genaro also chose to remain anchored to Paris, where he died during the Occupation, in early 1944. Juan Bautista Deambroggio, "Bachicha," whose orchestra Bianco-Bachicha had been so successful in Paris during the 20s, also remained faithful to the city, only ever returning to Buenos

Aires for visits, and more specifically Montparnasse, whose name graced one of the tangos he composed. Born in La Boca in 1890, he was still galvanizing the dance floor in the cellar of La Coupole, on Boulevard Montparnasse, when he died in 1963, a place where lay pilgrims, older and even elderly *milongueros*, turned out during those years prior to the rebirth of tango.)

GÜIRALDES KEEPS ON DANCING

There are no mistakes in tango . . . Not like life . . .
If you get all tangled up, you just tango on.

Al Pacino dancing in *Scent of a Woman*,
as Gardel sings *Por una cabeza*

Güiraldes's passion for tango dancing is evident in his first book, *El cencerro de cristal* (1915), which includes the poem "Tango" dated 1911, Paris. At the time, tango was first and foremost music meant for dancing, and that's how the writer relished in and practiced it.

Half a century later, in 1965, Ben Molar, a shrewd music industry entrepreneur, tango enthusiast (and scholar), songwriter for boleros and Spanish-language versions of North American and French songs, wanted to cut an LP. So he asked poets, visual artists, and musicians to come together to work on its composition and illustration. The result was titled *Catorce con el tango*. (From this call came the unexpected alliance, like a two-headed eagle, of Piazzolla and Borges.) Ulises Petit de Murat, along with several friends who had accompanied the remains of Güiraldes upon his death in Paris in 1929, from the port in Buenos Aires to San Antonio de Areco, partnered with Juan D'Arienzo in "Bailate un tango, Ricardo":

"I scrounge what I can from my life to stack against your death. / Life is only luck, after all, given by the delay / of half-dozy death and I rouse and so / I shout, shout out loud, come dance a tango, Ricardo! / (Ricardo Güiraldes dances and the angel of remembrance accompanies him / sending a crescent moon and a powerful shaft bridge / his seal over the slums of Buenos Aires that connects the Pampas and Tango.) / Dance a tango, Ricardo! Look who is shouting to you, / it's no silly matter, the kid's a bard, / the one from La Crencha Engrasada. De la Púa is asking you out now: / dance a tango, Ricardo! / (Ricardo Güiraldes dances his way out of life . . . / and in dancing leads, like the women before / drowsy death, who mutters lost in dreamy torpor / dance a tango, Ricardo.)"

Despite the heavy rhetoric, the lyrics matter because they evoke Güiraldes, consecrated early on for his novel, *Don Segundo Sombra*, as a dancer. In the memoir he wrote of his youthful years, Petit de Murat tells us: "Ricardo is about to leave for Europe. We saw him off with tango. El Malevo Muñoz, that Carlos de la Púa so corpulent yet as flexible as the fringe at the end of a piece of cloth, invites him out to dance a tango. There's an implicit challenge. Ricardo is supposed to outdo Malevo's figures. There's one in particular. Mid-step and without missing a beat, Malevo flung his shoes off into the distance without bending over to remove them, and went on like nothing had happened, triumphantly, dancing in his socks. It's hard for our beloved Ricardo to follow his move. Let's not hide the fact that everything is a little hard for him, despite his manliness, which precludes him from complaining. . . . Without metaphors: it's almost certain this was the last tango Güiraldes ever danced."

Victoria Ocampo, who so consistently celebrated Güiraldes following *Supremacía del alma y de la sangre* (1934), wasn't alone when, years later, she decided to leave a written trace of a different Güiraldes, the one she had spent time with as a girl: the "perfect" *milonguero*.

Odi et amo

One plays and sings other music to heal emotional
wounds, but one plays and sings the tango to
open wounds, so they stay open,
to remember them, to stick a finger into them . . .
Ramón Gómez de la Serna, *Interpretación del tango*

In "That Brothel Reptile" I tried to understand the historical and ideological reasons for the viciousness, the contempt, the feeling of affront to national pride and call to arms that gripped Argentine men and women of letters over European enthusiasm for tango dancing. And more intriguingly, I seem to detect in other writers a swing between fascination and repulsion like an overlay of transparencies.

Güiraldes's poem "Tango" is probably the first time tango dancing appeared in the "sophisticated" literature of Buenos Aires. (Borges rescues a fleeting mention in Carriego, but his poems, similar to Homero Manzi's lyrics a little later on, weren't immediately given a place in the canon.) Tango was a dance and only a dance until very late in the game. Though occasionally they might sing some lyrics, often written by a variety of different people for the same underlying score, these were largely droll, often impromptu, expressions savoring the improvised tradition of musical dialogues. Though Lola Candales debuted *La Morocha* on the 25th of December 1905 using lyrics written by Villoldo that very morning to Saborido's music, and though Villoldo himself had composed "El porteñito" two years earlier, the date usually cited to mark the first-ever tango song is January 3, 1917. That night, on stage at the Esmeralda Theater (now the Maipo), Gardel debuted "Mi noche triste" with Pascual Contursi's lyrics to a pre-existing composition by Samuel Castriota called "Lita," which only became popular thanks to the words given it by Contursi. (Like so much of the information gathered and commented on in these minutes, a shadow of a doubt hangs over the "tango song's" inaugural evening; the majority claim the debut took place in the Esmeralda while others set the stage at the Empire.)

What's at the center of Güiraldes's "Tango" is the dance, in its rough form, long before it was domesticated: a dance with a "thorny snigger of seduction" and the "breath of the brothel." Built like an impressionistic inventory, in the flavor of late decadence ("*La nostalgie de la boue*"), attraction and repulsion, both of them sensuous, thread together indistinguishably in his text:

Tango, miserable and severe.

Tango as menace.

Tango, whose every note falls hard and vindictive, below a hand truly meant for the handle of a knife.

Tragic tango, whose melody plays out the theme of enmity.

Slow rhythm, complex harmony with antagonistic contretemps.

Dance that fills with vertigos of virile exaltation, spirits clouded by drink.

Creator of silhouettes sashaying silently by, as if hypnotized by a bloody dream.

Brims of crooked hats above spiteful sneers.

The tyrant's all-absorbing love, jealous of his will to dominate.

Women delivered, under the thumb of obedient beasts.

Thorny snigger of seduction.

Breath of the brothel. Air that stinks of cheap broad and macho in the sweat of the fight.

Boding a sudden burst of shouts and threats that will end in a mute groan, a trickle of steamy blood, like the final rally of useless rage.

Red stain, coagulating black.

Fatal tango, haughty and crude.

Notes dragged, indolently, across a nasal keypad.

Tango, miserable and severe.

Tango as menace.

Dance of love and death.

The word "hypnotic" in Güiraldes's poem anticipates observations Martínez Estrada would capture decades later. In *Radiografía de la pampa* (1933) he captures a sense of the wariness, the distaste for these "bodies that remain fixed together, stuck, like insects copulating." The author acknowledges that in danced tango one finds an authentic expression of the "great village" of Buenos Aires.

The prophet saw the capital as a fragile veneer of civilization beneath which pulsated a never-overcome, always-lively savagery. Before his very eyes, the artificial city's music, ambushed and infiltrated by the infinite, displaced countryside, showed up as an "expressionless dance, monotonous, with the stylized rhythm of a city's administration. . . . It's a soulless dance, for automatons, for people that have renounced the complications of a life of the mind and opt for nirvana. It's a gliding. A dance of pessimism, the misfortune of all its members: a dance of the open plains, ever the same and of an anxious, subjugated race wandering endlessly on foot, without a destination, in the eternity of a repeating present."

Seven years later, in *La cabeza de Goliat*, it's the poet, no longer the prophet, who preaches blazing intuitions that reveal a precise understanding of something from which he nevertheless feels alienated: "Tango is not danced with the body, but with blood and soul. The soul of Buenos Aires is made flesh." And also: the bandoneon's "humid, gray-timbred voice, vibrant in its restrained and muscular lust."

Martínez Estrada identifies a melancholic quality not only in the *criollo* carnival, but also in the cabaret. His revelation of what is hidden is no less illuminating: "Even he who is joyful there, shows the joy of the cabaret. He has no habit of letting go, of diving into life as if it were water; he feels the embarrassment of never having been naked in front of other people, never swimming out to sea. Women, on the other hand, understand their obliged role and don't forget that they're rented out for this licentious comedy." It's the despair of the plains, it's relief-less landscape, seeping even into the city that had hoped to ignore it, defy it.

And it's through the cabaret that a defunct Buenos Aires, the city that birthed the first tango, disentombs it: "Nightfall is the time for secret societies and each observer behaves as a member of that sect of those who don't go to bed at ten." "Honest women who retire early only highlight the fact that the ones who stay on, are not." "Tango, nocturnal music, brings distress to these entertainment venues, because its cadence carries the remembrance of an abject past and voices stifled by dispossessed life."

In these, his most notable books ("poverty and ugliness crowd the gates of Buenos Aires, like beggars at the palace doors," *Radiografía de la pampa*), farsighted views alternate with rhetorical flourishes that feel dangerously close to Keyserling. If Martínez Estrada's essays continue to delight readers when so many other sociological treatises have been relegated to the dust of academic shelves, it's because his emotional intelligence cut through and subverted the purely intellectual: his prose, his ideas and opinions, are like provisional constructions, always ready to succumb to the intuition of a metaphor, because the poet grasps truth before the ideologue.

His *odi et amo* with tango is no more than the most passionate example of this association of opposites, in which rejection and attraction reach a volatile equilibrium, fecund thanks to its volatility, which he himself diagnosed as necessary ("what Sarmiento never saw") between civilization and savagery.

<hr/>

"I have a good description of the Santa Fe Palace in note cards kept in my files, whose name is not Santa Fe nor is it located on that street, but one nearby. It's a shame that none of it can really be described, not the modest façade with the promising posters and the shadowy box office. . . . What follows only gets worse, not that it's all bad because in those places there's nothing precise; but rather everything is in chaos, confusion rearranging itself into a false order: hell and its circles. A hell of a place like Parque Japonés at two-fifty a pop, ladies fifty cents."

The first person to suggest an approximation between the milonga and hell is the narrator of "The Gates of Heaven," a story from Julio Cortázar's collection *Bestiario* (1951) considered by many to be his best. The narrator is a lawyer who spends time with a modest couple, nearly dispossessed. Behind his intellectual curiosity, almost ethnographic, lies the nostalgia for strong experience, for a more intense and rudimentary life he's only felt vicariously, and translates into observations on language use and customs that he regularly transcribes on index cards. His desire is mediated by feelings of guilt over the inevitable distance with which he accepts their naïve trust, even respectful admiration on the part of this couple from whom he is separated by an invisible cultural wall: "It made me sick to my gut to think like that, for other people it's enough to feel that way, I have to think it."

During the lawyer's visit to the wake and then a milonga – in the story's Santa Fe Palace one can recognize the famous Enramada, stomping grounds of soldiers and maids in the mid-20th century – Cortázar narrates a story of "love and death" superimposed, interwoven with an analysis of the narrator's incapacity, at once remorseful and smug, to feel along with the characters in the story, admired precisely for possessing a gift he doesn't have. In the story it's the cultural more than the social distance that advances to extremes of lust and rejection, which repeatedly crystallize around the dance and the ambiance of the milonga: "when all the bandoneons struck out at once, a renewed violence overcame the dance, a scramble of lateral runs and entwined figure eights in the middle of the floor. Many were sweating, a *china* (a woman of mixed Indian race), about the height of my jacket's second button, passed by the table and I saw the sweat oozing from the roots of her hair and running down the nape of her neck where a roll of fat made an even whiter crease."

"The Gates of Heaven" has been studied beside Borges and Bioy Casares's story, "The Monster's Feast," as being symptomatic of a classist reaction to the first Peronist era, or more likely one based on education levels. It's a plausible approach, though Cortázar's story, more than anything else, is like a session of necromancy sparked by the oldest of human desires, to recuperate a loved one who has passed. The text's intelligence can be found in how the plot is held suspended, at once mythical and yet grounded, inviting us to perceive a second storyline: one of the intellectual who feels inadequate when faced with an experience that eludes analysis. This strategy of an impossible dialogue between passion and distance reinforces the myth: the narrator knows the dead cannot return ("I was standing still, coolly smoking a cigarette, watching him come and go, he knew that he was wasting his time, that he would come back tired and thirsty, not having found the gates of heaven among all that smoke and all those people") yet he can't help but admire and deliver an ending to the man who opens a path through the milonga dancing couples to look for his dearly departed.

In "The Gates of Heaven," as in other selected *odi et amo* in diverse discursive registers, we find the insights of writers and intellectuals who, while sensitive to the dance's seductive appeal, probably never actually danced it themselves, bar Güiraldes. Their work is like a breadcrumb trail that draws out a somewhat perplexed, almost artful fascination: they can't evade tango, but neither can they give themselves over to it. That kind of incongruity runs completely contrary to the staunch distaste Roberto Arlt felt for the dance. In an oft-cited remark, Cortázar pointed out how scarce the allusions are to tango in Arlt's books, "always with a clear undercurrent of contempt and revulsion," as if hoping to distance himself from the poverty where he saw himself reflected.

An eloquent example of that revulsion appears in one of the most alarmist of Arlt's texts, "Las fieras," from his collection *The Little Hunchback* (1933). A jaunt into the universe of the brothels in the Province of Buenos Aires, the story, brimming with reminiscences of German expressionism in its harsh brushstrokes and schematic contours, plays on the naïve conviction that one can find something particularly authentic in the typecasts of "hard living": "An old tango reminds us of a spell in prison, or to others the night they found a woman, or to others a terrible time walking on the seedy side. If tango turns jagged, a spasm cramps our soul. Then you remember the rotten, red gratification of smashing a woman's face in with a fist or, too, the pleasure of dancing braided together with a cagey dame in a murderous milonga, or the first money the woman who initiated us in life gave us, a ten peso bill plucked from her garter received with trembling joy because she earned that money bedding others."

From Güiraldes's rather naïve fascination with the self-satisfied truculence of Arlt, through Martínez Estrada's dying attempt to come to terms with contradictory feelings, or the intellectual playfulness of Cortázar's narrative detachments, what's telling is the music, the dance, and the atmosphere that infuses them. In these variations on the subject of tango, one can read into each one a reflection of the literary persona the writer has chosen to, or perhaps only has agreed to, embody.

Piringundines

It's midnight, the cabaret rouses.
Lots of women, flowers and champagne . . .
The sad, eternal party is about to begin
for those who live to the rhythm of gotán.
Juan Carlos Marambio Catán, Acquaforte

One afternoon in 1952, León Benarós shows up ("not without a bit of excitement") at number 2721 of Carlos Calvo Street. He takes a photograph of the patio, chipped and peeling, where a door separates the house from the street, an inner door decorated with wrought iron arabesques and filigrees, a trace of bygone aspirations; several rooms frame the patio, wooden shutters closed tight, doors crowned by ornamental cornices. Ivy hangs over metal arches, only partially covering them with its benevolent shadow. The house seems not to have undergone renovations since 1900, back when the street was called Europa. In its day, the residence had been a *locus classicus* in the history of milonga: "María la Vasca's place."

The poet acknowledges the ghosts who come out to greet him.

I knew that Ponzio, "*El Pibe*" Ernesto, who composed the tango "Don Juan," had played violin there, accompanied on the flute by Vicente "*El Tano*" Pecci. Benarós recalls them with particular tenderness, though he's aware that the musician who left the greatest mark of all was the bandoneonist Vicente Greco, who composed "Rodríguez Peña" and "Racing Club." Greco had anticipated Fresedo's foresight, becoming a successful musician among a "high society" that began welcoming tango into its ballrooms after taking it for a coy first spin: "He's the golden boy of the upper crust families. He performed in the Plaza Hotel, the home of doctor Lucio V. López (Callao just shy of the corner of Quintana Avenue), at Green's, at Lagos García's, and Lamarque's, among others. Gigs like that fetch 200 dollars minimum."

By contrast, the house prompts Benarós to recall another, very different residence. He had never been there, but its legend had spread far and wide: known as "Laura's," it was a sumptuous ballroom, located at Paraguay 2512." Rosendo Mendizábal, "*El Pardo Rosendo*," who debuted in 1897 with "El entrerriano," was the presiding pianist for a "highlife" clientele. "At Laura's Place," with lyrics by Cadícamo and music by Antonio Polit, is a tango that conjures up those evenings:

At the milonga at Laura's
I danced with dark Flora . . .
A milonga so provocative
it left an aura . . .
Ah . . . the milonga at Laura's . . .

And another, *El porteñito*, is also evocative of those times (lyrics by Carlos Pesce for music composed much earlier, in 1903, by Villoldo). In 1933, in full nostalgia for those olden times, and with all the distances between Laura's and La Vasca's now gone by the wayside, they both appear in a verse of "No aflojés," lyrics by Mario Battistella to music by Maffia y Piana.

Perhaps these two matrons are the first ghosts to come and visit the poet that afternoon.

Laura's name was Laurentina Montserrat. The visitor describes her as being tall, dark-haired, distinguished, with an accent that might possibly be from Mendoza; he'd heard about her generosity towards less prosperous relatives, her respectable season tickets to South America's greatest opera house, the Colón, a taste for showing off her jewelry in the soirées she presided over in "Buenos Aires barely woken from the lethargy of colonial boredom" (Benarós). Keeping tabs on her daughter's education and behavior, she had her "nearly sequestered" on the upper floors of the house, far from the mirrors and French furniture, from the polar bear head and pelt over an always gleaming salon floor, and from the "drawn-out bed" of the maternal boudoir, with its canopy and fur covering. Married to somebody named Sosa, Laura finagled a way not to discourage her tenacious admirer, commissioner of the 21st District, to whom Mendizábal dedicated his tango "Don Enrique."

Benarós doesn't give María la Vasca's legal name – she was María Rongalla – though he describes her as being "full-faced, nearly plump, but well shaped," which means far from Laura's probably studied elegance. An anonymous spectator once called in to a television program after hearing him describe her. "Listen, I'm married, a woman of a certain age, and my husband doesn't like me to talk about such things. But my mother was a close friend of María la Vasca's. She told me she used to wear a simple dress around the house, of raw silk with buttons made of pounds sterling . . ." Benarós thinks this private ostentation could be read as a form of payback for who-knows-what kind of penuries past.

———

The city's dance hall welcomed
the "corporal drama" of its inhabitants and
those who never learned to walk in two-four time
were doomed to being disoriented,
uprooted, and strangers unto themselves.

Christian Ferrer, "Danza macabra"

Were these dance halls really clandestine brothels? Mere "schools" where by drawing on discretion, not haggling particulars, and in tacit cahoots, it was possible to "go further" if one so chose?

The classical image of two *guapos* dancing in a corner, written into verse by Carriego and depicted by the painter Héctor Basaldúa, is part of the mythical origin of the dance: it coincides with a time when vacant lots were cleared of weeds and the earth was pounded to allow for dancing. When did they start to proliferate and in what order, the slave yard repurposed, the tenement patio, the first bashful public dance halls in the neighborhoods? When they were designated "schools," *academias*, it was less to crown a transformation than because the rite's primitive stages aspired to something more. Their most prestigious avatar, the cabaret, would be seen retrospectively, years after vanishing, as a "public and ceremonial version of the age-old brothel" (Blas Matamoro).

In María la Vasca's, it was Charles Kern (Carlos el Inglés), the owner's companion, physically intimidating and a reputable dancer, who was put in charge of keeping crowds in line, making sure people behaved and safeguarding the establishment's decorum. In the early part of the 20th century, clients paid twenty pesos for a bottle of French champagne, two for a beer. The musicians were paid five pesos apiece at the end of the night. The girls, dressed in their finery and not street clothes, arrived around eleven in open cars known as "victorias"; they were paid three pesos per hour danced and La Vasca called them in according to the number of male dancers who had reserved spots.

Despite the difference in their levels of elegance, both Laura's and María la Vasca's were priced above the pockets of the general public. Benarós inherited stories passed down by word of mouth, memories of other dance halls, much more modest ones, where a more explicit form of commerce may have been available: there was China Rosa's, Doña Augusta's, Elvira Lastra's, La Vieja Eustaquia's, and La Parda Adelina's. And a step farther down was the old store-house at Tano 43, in Villa Crespo.

Yet these establishments were characterized by a level of urbanity very far from the origins of tango dancing. The myth would have us believe that around 1880, at Los Corrales Viejos, near Caseros and Rioja, a transformation took place wherein the original milonga still connected to rural music, was converted into the lower-class, urban tango from the outskirts. The areas around the slaughterhouses, prior to the ones in Liniers, were full of bars where the cowhands, once freed of the livestock they wrangled into the city, would drink, make music, and dance.

Did they also dance in the *cuartos de las chinas* (quarters of young underclass women of mixed Indian blood, not necessarily prostitutes but who cavort with soldiers) near the military barracks in Palermo? The Military School and the first Artillery regiment were located from 1870 to 1892 on land that had belonged to the strongman Juan Manuel de Rosas, near his residence in San Benito de Palermo; and same as anywhere, at any time, barracks breed brothels: in this particular case, this school, this regiment, brought a proliferation of ranches to the area; and hence the so-called *chinas cuarteleras* catered to the immediate needs of low-ranking officers and soldiers. And what about the Carpas de la Batería neighborhood beside the Retiro, in what is today the very upscale hill where Florida Street ends, in front of San Martín Square? The precarious outfits that sprung up in the area, meant to quickly satisfy a very precise urge, had no need for musical preludes, and even less the danceable kind, given the form of recreation on offer.

Yet a sort of effluvium of the defunct "wild life" lingered in that gardened area of Palermo. The Restaurante del Parque Tres de Febrero, a tea house by day and a spot for partying hordes by night, was located at the intersection of what is today Sarmiento and Figueroa Alcorta Avenues, at Los Portones de Palermo, the iron gates built to mark the entrance to the park, or simply called "Los Portones." The restaurant, inaugurated in 1875, was demolished in 1912 and went down in tango history as Hansen's, after the last name of the Swedish man who ran it. (Other venues in the area of Los Portones – El Belvedere, El Tambito, El Quisquito – experienced the same metamorphosis between the diurnal and the nocturnal clientele.)

The memoirists contradict each other in this case, too. According to some, Hansen was German, not Swedish. The most widely accepted legend says that "Hansen's" was a milonga-dancing scene where *cocottes* and *chinas cuarteleras*, *guapos*, *niños bien*, and off-duty military men gathered but didn't mix. They'd have rivaled proprietorship over women and levels of pluck in those frugally lit spaces decorated with colored lanterns. Of a random night, two famous milonga dancers would have fought a duel of cuts and breaks: El Cachafaz for Abasto, and El Pardo Santillán for Palermo, with victory claimed by the former. According to other accounts, there was no dance floor to speak of. No one was seen dancing on a tiled floor in a central patio, and if on the occasional night a stray couple practiced a few steps on the flattened earth of the pathways between groves and *reservées*, it's not something that made Hansen's a dancing venue.

I prefer to trust my inner Virgil and guide myself towards places less worked over by legend.

———

Benarós turns to the authority of Francisco Romay, amateur historian, retired commissioner. According to Romay, in its origin, the *piringundín* (a type of honky-tonk milonga) was a sort of watering hole where men danced alone. Later they came to be called "bailongos." When women began frequenting them to dance, a gradual process of climbing up the hierarchy ocurred, which ended in the cabaret. Benarós cites Romay extensively, though he prefers to disregard the chronicler's etymological narrative regarding the origin of the word "piringundín": a Paraguayan guitar player whose last name was Piris or Pirín, and a Brazilian accordionist, José Pérez Gundín, used to perform in a tavern in Riachuelo when the ships docked there on layovers.

For however unlikely this hypothesis seems, and of course it's unverifiable, it's still more plausible than the one suggested by the scholars Barcia and Gobello, which Benarós accepted despite being so utterly *recherché*: the name must derive from the French region, Perigord, and its folkloric dance, the *périgourdine*. . . . How the term ever came to impose itself on the shores of the Río de la Plata, and the itinerary of its descent, is something the authors don't bother to explain. And it's the one thing that leaves the avid reader hanging on the edge.

For this same reader, though, nothing could be more extravagant than the names of some of the milonga dancers of the heroic times: La Parda Refucilo, La Fosforito, Pepa la Chata, La Guanaca, La Tanita Luciana, Lola la Petiza, La Mondonguito, La Payaso, La China Venicia, María la Tero, La Sargento, and the prestigious Carmen Gómez, and Parda Flora, and the highly renowned Blonde Mireya, mentioned in the lyrics of the famous tango "Tiempos viejos" (lyrics by Manuel Romero and music by Francisco Canaro), and another, less familiar tango, composed by Augusto Gentile.

(For Héctor Ángel Benedetti, Blonde Mireya never existed in "real" life; she was a fictional character that belonged to the corpus of the diverse creatures of milonga. Even her name derives from the French Mireille, the title of a poem by Frédéric Mistral – "Mirèio" in the original Provençal (Langue d'Oc), later adapted for the libretto of Gounod's opera. Two years before he composed the lyrics for "Tiempos viejos," Manuel Romero had given the name

Mireya to the main character of a comic sketch *El rey del cabaret*, which he wrote together with Alberto Weisbach. A journalist decided to stoke the traditional rivalry that exists between the two shores of the Río de la Plata over the origin of tango and Gardel's nationality, and suggested that the personality's real name was Margarita Verdier, also known as "La Oriental" because she was born in Uruguay . . .)

My favorite nicknames: La Barquinazo, a lame woman who, dancing a strict two-four time, gave a very singular style to her figures thanks to her physical limitations, and Sarita Bicloruro, survivor of two failed suicide attempts by chemical mixtures.

Back to Benarós, from whom I inherit testimonies that the poet, in turn, inherited from Domingo Greco. The most celebrated dancers around 1900 were Vitulo, El Tano Ponce, Cotongo, and "La Vieja" Pedrín, "who brought tango to its maximum level of refinement." For Pancho Panelo, a *niño bien*, poise was his most distinguished feature: he could dance with a glass of champagne on his head without spilling a drop. Another of his kind, El Maco (Mariano) Milani, squandered his fortune in the milongas. El Flaco Saúl, El Cívico, El Flaco Alfredo, El Moscovita, El Tarila (Giuseppe Giambuzzi), Bernabé Simara, El Nene del Abasto, El Pibe Palermo (José María Baña), La Lora (Egidio Scarpino), El Escoberito. And I include some of the more recent tango dancers: the incomparable Petróleo (Carlos Estévez) and El Rusito Elías (Elías Borovsky).

Casimiro Aín, "El Vasco" or "El Lecherito," was the first to dance tango in Paris, in 1913, if not earlier; he died in Buenos Aires in 1940, having been on crutches for months after his leg was amputated due to a failed operation. Seventy years after Aín's Paris debut, Virulazo (Jorge Martín Orcalzaguirre) would also dance a tango in Paris, the evening that signaled the passionate rebirth of tango on an international scale: November, 1983, the night *Tango argentino* debuted, on stage at the Châtelet.

My favorite person: El Cachafaz (Benito, or Ovidio José, Bianquet) because he died in a milonga one night in 1942, in the arms of Carmencita Calderón. (What do I care if someone would correct me saying he died backstage after dancing with her in Bahía Blanca? He died in a milonga, in a dimension of the milonga, which banishes any insouciant documentary exactitude.)

———

*"Chère madame, de mon temps cela ne
se faisait qu'au lit."*
> The princess of Metternich to the wife of the
> Argentine Ambassador while watching a tango

"Est-ce qu'on est censé le danser debout?"
> The Countess of Pourtalès upon seeing
> a tango danced for the first time

*. . . the closest thing you'll find to a vertical
expression of a horizontal desire.*

Angela Rippon

The tangos danced in brothels all sported explicit titles: *Dos sin sacar, Metele bomba al Primus, Empugá que se va a abrir, La c . . . ara de la l . . . una, Date vuelta, Se te paró el motor, Embadurname la persiana, Afeitate el 7 que el 8 es fiesta, Dejalo morir adentro* . . . The title *Queco* is either the ground zero of wit, or the summit of sloth: the word used to be a synonym for brothel; *Dame la lata* (Give me the tin) (according to several sources, the first documented tango: 1888) alludes to the metal chip the patron used to pay his turn, which the prostitute would later hand over to the madame or her pimp as proof of the done deed.

We can read the double entendre between the dance hall and the brothel in the title *Dame la lata*: the man bought one or several tin chips to be given to the milonga dancer also in the "*bailetín*," the "school" or the café that was full of "*camareras*" (waitresses), all of whose services were gauged by the number of tins per dance. On the other hand, in nearly all bordello salons, first came the dancing, and then the man could bring the chosen prostitute "to the *piezas*" or the bedroom area (*pieza* can mean a musical piece or dance, or also bedroom). Sergio Mendizábal, Rosendo's brother who composed "El entrerriano," performed at Concepción Amaya's establishment on Lavalle 2177; when the madame had to leave the capital for Nueve de Julio, she brought the musician along with her.

The danceable music flowed into the streets from Balvanera to San Cristóbal despite the jealously fastened shutters of the city's countless "houses of ill repute." It was less aggressive than a woman exhibiting herself in a doorframe on Pichincha Street during the golden age of Rosario's Sunchales barrio, more insinuating than the occasional whistle from behind the shutters on Junín and Viamonte in Buenos Aires; now a two-four time sent passersby the tacit promises that only wordless music can infer.

Could it be heard outside the most truculent houses in the barely developed outskirts at the beginning of the 20th century: San Fernando, Florencio Varela, even the ones in Ensenada? Those were the days when maritime traffic was burgeoning and everything along the "lower" areas of Buenos Aires, from Retiro to Riachuelo, was given over to the "wild life." There are accounts of two different opium dens in La Boca, for satisfying the urges of Oriental crews, and the curiosity of straying rich kids. And of course there was El Farol Colorado on Maciel Island, which Manuel Gálvez describes in *Historia del arrabal* as a scene of regular brawling among rowdy sailors awash in alcohol and pornographic "eyefuls." Exactly which of the dance halls abided by what their names announced?

Juan Santa Cruz told Benarós about a certain house where dancing would have been unequivocally impossible. An independent prostitute, bearer of a promising name, Juana Rebenque (riding crop), lived in the so-called Barrio de las Ranas or El Bañado, which today is called Nueva Pompeya, or New Pompeii, in "a tin house, so small . . . You had to squat to enter. She had no fixed rate. She charged what they gave her. She never came to downtown."

The cabaret slowly but surely tidied itself up through the 30s and 40s, though the "low life" reputation from its early years took some time to shed. In *El veneno del tango* (1927), Valentín de Pedro's "novel for the stage," the cabaret is what leads the young *criollos* to ruin. Yet in opposition to his extremely moralizing intentions, there is Edmo Cominetti's film, *La borrachera del tango*, light-hearted and good-natured, tiptoeing through the code of "good manners," it reassures the cabaret's prestige as part of a life of merriment, champagne and stimulants. Perhaps the ultimate image of the cabaret, at once realistic and legendary, can be found in the lyrics to the famous tango "Acquaforte," lyrics by Juan Carlos Marambio Catán to Horacio Pettorossi's musical score:

> *It's midnight. The cabaret awakens.*
> *Lots of women, flowers and champagne.*
> *The eternal, the sad party is about to begin*
> *for those who live by the rhythm of gotán (tango).*

Chained by forty years of life
my white head, old heart:
today I see full of pity
what before I saw with glee.

Poor milongas,
intoxicated by kisses,
they look at me estranged,
out of curiosity.
They no longer know me:
I'm old and alone,
no twinkle in my eyes . . .
Life slips away . . .

"An old lecher spending his money
getting Lulú drunk on champagne
today he denied a poor laborer his raise
who asked him for another chunk of bread.
That poor woman selling flowers
in my day the queen of Montmartre
offers me violets with a smile
to ease, perhaps, my loneliness.

"And I think about life:
the mothers who suffer,

> *the children who wander*
> *without a roof or piece of bread,*
> *selling La Prensa,*
> *earning two cents . . .*
> *How sad it all is!*
> *I'd like to cry!"*

Marambio Catán (1895–1973) left a book of memoirs that allows us to follow his ill-fated career as a folk singer, repertoire actor, author of one of the lyrics attached to the tango *El choclo*, soloist in orchestras on tour through Europe and Egypt with Julio de Caro and Eduardo Bianco; he retired at forty-eight, after singing and acting in one of Samuel Eichelbaum's plays. The "Acquaforte" score came out of a visit he made to the Excelsior Cabaret in Milan with Pettorossi, in 1931 or 1932. To be able to play there, the Fascist regime's censor required them to clearly state that the tango was an Argentine form, which responds to an Argentine reality: in Mussolini's Italy, the censors adduced, there were no such pathetic social contrasts or profligate customs. It was debuted by the tenor Gino Franci.

Beyond the anecdote, the Argentine character present in "Acquaforte" would seem exemplary. The lyrics are suffused by a very lucid sensibility that is free of rebelliousness and resigned to the tragic social landscape. Far from the threats in *¡Se viene la maroma!* (1928, lyrics by Manuel Romero to Enrique Delfino's musical score, "maroma" alludes to a revolution or an upheaval), with its naïve – perhaps realistic? – vision of the aspirations of classes that today would be called "dispossessed": "The Soviet storm is brewing. / The convicts are tired of eating bread and salami / today they want oysters with sweet Sautern and champagne." It also detaches itself from the more realistic panorama of strikes, repression and jailing that can be found in *Al pie de la Santa Cruz* (1933, lyrics by Mario Battistella, also to Deflino's music).

What matters about "Acquaforte" to a book not focused on tango as music but as a dance is its subjective, if disenchanted, view regarding the pleasures – so come-hither in the old days – of a milonga night. Though the personalities and situations it evokes have become commonplaces of international cinema, they draw a perfect synthesis of the *loci classici* associated with the cabaret in Buenos Aires: the man who comes back "browbeaten," the milongas "crazy for the *pris*" (from *prises*, cocaine), the "saintly older woman." Wavering between *odi et amo*, the two intellectual poles of love and hate, "Acquaforte" strikes an emotional balance, indulgent towards the world of the cabaret and the guilty pleasure, which is key for evoking it with a bit of amusement or joy.

⁓

Besides the cabaret, there were also dance halls whose regular clients couldn't be more unlike the ones that frequent today's milongas: men went on their own, to dance with mercenary companions, or women employed as house servants. (I don't know of a single Argentine film that has portrayed these young female dancers whose cadenced company was renewed by purchasing a ticket, the way they have been in so many American films of the 30s and 40s.)

The only example among Argentine writers is that of Estela Canto, who left written testimony of her reflections on dancing tango and her own experiences in these halls. Her testament is doubly valuable: for being written by a woman, perhaps the only one at the time to describe her own particular experience with tango, and because she was actually employed as an occasional dancer in one of the halls in Buenos Aires. It's unheard of, at least among Borges's group of friends.

Canto avoids any philosophical speculation regarding the dance, any intellectual detachment; there is neither denunciation nor desire in her words: "The tango of cuts is quick and complicated, with twisted arabesques in nearly the same spot; brusque advances and then sudden standstills for no apparent reason; motionless for a few seconds, as if in concentration, only to begin that triggered march again, that complex weave, that movement of advance inevitably interrupted, cut. . . So we come face to face with perhaps one of the unique characteristics of tango: it's a dance where the pass is abruptly interrupted, where the rhythm is halted like a startled horse reined in."

Hugo Beccacece recalls: "In an unpublished interview with Canto before she passed, she told me that before she met Borges and became a translator (she spoke English quite well) and a journalist, she'd worked at many odd jobs. During a particularly difficult time, for example, she had been 'for hire' as a dancer in select dance halls, where a man could buy several tickets that would give him access to the array of girls employed by the venue. Dressed as 'milonguitas' in tight skirts with a slit up the side, the girls were expected to move across the dance floor to the beat of a foxtrot or tango. Estela lasted only three days at the job. She told me about the experience in our conversation: "It was a clandestine form of prostitution. Some girls, after the dance, would leave the venue and go off with one of their dance partners. I wouldn't. So I wasn't very popular with the clients: they immediately realized that all I would do was dance. No concessions. What's more, I didn't like to be forced to dance with men who were often fat, nearly prehistoric, and clumsy.'"

—

We slip through serene ruins
that had once been famous Italica . . .
let us commit the act of shadows
over the ivy on the stages.

J. R. Wilcock, "Epithalamium"

Ubi sunt . . . The Tabaris was raised where the Royal Pigalle had been, on Corrientes between Esmeralda and Suipacha Streets. In the early

30s of last century, an English traveler came to the conclusion that "it is an education in the tango to have heard *Por qué* at Tabaris." The Casanova and the Marabú faced each other on Maipú Street between Corrientes and Sarmiento, and there was the Bambú on Corrientes and Maipú . . . Tibidabo was on the other side of the Obelisco, on Corrientes between Libertad and Talcahuano, and the Chanteclair a little further along on Paraná between Corrientes and Lavalle, which at some point was called Vieux Paris because its façade was an imitation of the Moulin Rouge . . .

Most of these cabarets lasted through the mid 50s. Which is longer than the cabarets in El Bajo (Montmartre, Royal, Ocean Dancing, Derby, Cielo de California) and La Boca (Charleston, Avión), with their rougher clientele of sailors of all origins. If these venues were doomed by the gradual decrease of maritime traffic, the cabarets downtown, with their varying degrees of elegance, were eclipsed by the public's changing tastes, the trends in entertainment, perhaps a gradual liberalizing of customs that would drive sexuality into the light or the shadows, but no longer in collusion with the penumbras.

In the 40s and early 50s, the only thing keeping the link with the archaic *piringundín* alive were the "*alternadoras*" (women meant for company, not necessarily anything more) also called "*coperas*" (from *copa*, which means glass; drinking companions). After dancing with a client, the girls would get themselves invited to his table for a drink. As the waiter filled and refilled his glass of whisky, they would fill and refill an identical glass for the girls, but of tea, to keep them awake and alert, cheerfully observing the client's blossoming tab. An older "copera," out of professional circulation, would supervise the ladies' *toilette*; acting as confidante and counselor, the active girls would usually call her Mami or Mamita. At the end of the evening, the pimp or "protector" would come round to pick up his cut and accompany them home.

I never had the chance to frequent one of these "temples of nocturnal life," whose rituals, though, I conjured in a story. I know the alternative for the true milonga dancers was the neighborhood "sport's club," with its family-based clientele, vigilant over the conduct of maiden daughters, over decorum in manners and embraces . . . I wonder what young people today might think, who go to the milongas from that latent world, the one that still beats deep inside the music they're dancing to. The power of what is absent is always stronger the farther away it is from the surface of experience. Perhaps an inclination for becoming a "copera" or "cafisho" (pimp) lurks unawares inside these young milonga dancers: a make-believe, alternate identity that could save them briefly from the banality of everyday life.

(With enough distance, a certain perfume of the novelesque winds up redeeming what had been sordid in its day, steeping it in what Benjamin diagnosed as a "leftist melancholy" [*Linksmelancholie*]. Weill's *Dreigroschenoper*, and Brecht watched how the left's critical edge waned over the years, its caustic parody, till it became a beacon of dubious nostalgia, like Berlin's for the Weimar Republic: the unprecedented freedom from mores or customs at the time, along with the fizzy, sparkling *show business* and cultural life, has kept from retrospective scrutiny all the coeval hunger and desperation. The historical *fatum* that period of time was meant to bury, and with such violence, adds a little zing of danger whenever it's evoked.)

Steps, attitudes, the embrace, and closed eyelids allow one to live a fiction, to act out as characters in a fleeting novel that nevertheless expresses something that's true, that is no less authentic for being imaginary. Dancing tango puts the adamant, indomitable potency of desire on stage.

I would like to bid farewell to this book by returning to the words of Ezequiel Martínez Estrada: "Perhaps no other music lends itself to reverie like tango. It enters your being and possesses it wholly, like a narcotic. Its rhythm allows you to suspend thought, and frees the soul to float inside the body . . ."